Eugène Ionesco

Eugène Ionesco

AMÉDÉE

THE NEW TENANT

VICTIMS OF DUTY

Translated by Donald Watson

GROVE PRESS, INC.   NEW YORK

First Grove Press Edition 1958

Ninth Printing

Manufactured in the United States of America

Three plays by

Eugène Ionesco

CONTENTS

RETROSPECT

EUGÈNE IONESCO has written in the Foreword to Volume I*
of the two states of consciousness in which his plays have their
origin, two contrasting yet similar impressions that the ordinary,
everyday world has changed its nature. Both the objects we
find in real life and the words we use seem to him, at one
extreme to become more rarefied, at the other to proliferate, and
grow dense and heavy with matter. The one state promises
escape, the other enslaves. Both experiences testify to the unreality
of our 'real' world.

To communicate this experience dramatically Ionesco starts
by showing us familiar characters in a familiar world—usually
presented in a familiar theatrical convention—and then lets the
unfamiliar erupt through the picture until it disintegrates and
we are faced with an illogical world, which has an alarming and
unfamiliar logic of its own.

Ionesco's treatment of story and situation, properties and set,
character and emotion is all of a piece. Each element reflects the
dynamic tension of his world: a world in which the familiar
and the unfamiliar, the logical and the illogical coexist but never
correspond. All this is expressed organically in the author's
language.

Just as *Victims of Duty* reveals something of Ionesco's approach
to drama, so *The Lesson*, both implicitly and explicitly, demon-
strates his attitude towards words. There he makes it clear that
for him words gain in significance as they lose in meaning.
Luckily, as they do so, they also tend to make us laugh. Ionesco's
style often produces comedy, but it does much more than that.

Mention of some of the problems that arose in translating
these plays may help to throw some light on Ionesco's use of
language.

Perhaps the main point of interest was the discovery that his
treatment varies quite distinctly from one play to the next. Mixed

*From *Cahiers des Quatre Saisons*, No. I, 1955

in different proportions in each play are the following styles, which we might call: banality, exaggeration (to include repetition and inconsequence), illogicality, dislocation and elevation.

The first, which I am taking to be roughly equivalent to ordinary conversation, is perhaps the basic style and can be found in all the plays. But our everyday platitudes and common-places have been enlivened in various ways, and these I shall consider later. These special uses apart, banality is employed almost all through *The New Tenant*, in most of *Amédée* and in something like half of *Victims of Duty*. Some banalities are funny in themselves, but when used, as they are in the first two plays, to point a contrast between the strangeness of the action and a response normally reserved for familiar happenings, they can be highly amusing, and darkly significant as well. As an example, one could cite Amédée's attempt to console Madeleine for the fantastic plight they are in with the words: 'Everyone has problems'. Here it would seem to be the translator's job to find the equivalent banalities of everyday conversation in his own language, without straining too pedantically after the exact form of the original.

Then Ionesco makes these banalities more interesting by varying the way they are used. Sometimes this simply takes the form of repetition: Amédée's 'I must get down to it', or the Old Woman's 'Did you put your pullover on?'. Sometimes they seem more striking because they appear out of place in their context: many of the proverbial remarks in *The Bald Prima Donna* are perfectly normal in themselves; they amuse us by their irrelevance, their inconsequence. Or he may use a special tech-nique to produce a similar effect, as in *Amédée*, when the voices of husband and wife cross, Amédée ordering groceries at the window, Madeleine dictating over the telephone.

Next there comes some form of illogicality. A characteristic example in *The Bald Prima Donna* is the time it takes to go through the family history of the lady 'who used sometimes in winter, just like everyone else, to catch a cold'. This play is full of illogical, almost surrealistic, humour: 'You may sit down on the chair, when the chair hasn't any', or 'I'd rather see a bird in a field than a marrow in a wheelbarrow'. It is full of verbal fun, puns and nonsense. Occasionally we find language being used in a similar way in *The Lesson*: the Professor's reminiscence of his friend, the viscount. In *Jacques* the same technique is used, but to more serious purpose: I need only mention, in the final episode between Jacques and Roberta II, the sexually significant play on the French word '*chat*', to which ultimately all language is reduced.

This kind of language is a fascinating nightmare for a translator, full of pitfalls. One can only go on revising, polishing, and hoping. Ionesco seems to have used *The Bald Prima Donna* as an experiment in verbal technique: it is more a question of finding equivalents in one's own language than of making a straightforward translation, and the danger is that one may get carried away. An additional problem is the fact that this play is set in England and has some details that seem uncharacteristic to an English audience, and some references that are too specifically French: these, of course, had to be changed. This is not surprising when we realise that Ionesco had never been to England at the time: he found most of his inspiration in the Assimil Method of learning English. Though it must not be forgotten he has said that if he had been learning Spanish, the play would have been set in Spain.

When we come to *Jacques* and *The Chairs* we find language being pushed a stage further: towards dislocation. In *The Chairs* it happens at two particular moments: first, the Old Couple's story, so familiar to them that a few detached syllables are enough to induce helpless laughter; and then the moment when the conversation between them dies and syntax falls apart. In *Jacques* the whole verbal texture of the play has become so thin in logical, so rich in associational meaning, that it only just carries the burden of the 'plot'. Words are invented, telescoped or deformed: words like 'chronometrable', 'eulogue', 'aristocroot', 'abracchante', 'mononster'. And sometimes words run away with the dialogue, one calling up another regardless of normal sense, as in the little scene between Jacques and his sister. There is a great deal of assonance, alliteration and rhyme.

Jacques is a more difficult play to translate than *The Bald Prima Donna* because of the sheer density of the verbal play, and because of its stronger 'plot'. The need to keep this 'plot' in evidence narrows the range of possible English equivalents to render the key words. One must sacrifice neither sound nor sense. Fearing this, I remember asking Ionesco once what was the point of one or two specially puzzling remarks in *Jacques*. 'None at all', he said, 'that *is* the point. Put anything you like.' But the trouble is 'anything' does not always have the same effect. There is one line in *The Bald Prima Donna* that illustrates this difficulty: 'No, she thought it was her comb' (a direct translation). Everyone wants to cut or change this line. But in fact it often raises a laugh. The audience is meant to ask: 'What was that? Did he say *comb*?' There is here no sound pattern to guide you. It seems best in such cases to keep as close as possible to the original.

So far, the illustrations considered have contributed mostly to the humour of the plays. But Ionesco also uses the elevated style. When he wishes to convey his vision of 'muddy slime' or 'airy splendour', his vocabulary becomes more conventionally romantic and a new regularity of rhythm heightens the effect: Amédée gazing at the night sky, the Professor carried away by language, Roberta II and Jacques in their verbal evocation of a sexual encounter, and Choubert descending into the depths or climbing the mountain into space. A large part of *Victims of Duty* is written in this style.

Ionesco also has a less conventional way of giving a poetic dimension to his prose: he increases its density by playing carefully and often unostentatiously on rhyme, assonance and alliteration. He employs this technique most in *The Chairs*, and in parts of *Victims of Duty*, but more discreetly than in *Jacques* or *The Bald Prima Donna* and without comic intent.

It is interesting to note how much less this style is used in *Amédée*, *The New Tenant* and *The Lesson*. It is the most difficult of all to render into English without sacrificing the simple rhythm and vocabulary.

I need hardly add that these two methods of elevating the style are exclusive neither of one another nor of the other aspects we have considered. Naturally none of these styles are as separate as I may have made them appear, but it is true that the predominance of one or other helps to give each play its peculiar flavour.

Sometimes these plays have been found too long, but very often when a producer wanted to cut them I realized the fault was mine. The plays in this edition have not been cut.

The translation of a personal idiom of this kind presents many difficulties. One has constantly to weigh the rival claims of sense, accuracy, rhythm, rhyme, assonance, and alliteration, and the first two do not, and I am convinced should not, always tip the scales. Where it seemed to me that the words themselves, more than the idea in the author's mind, were dictating the language, I have tried to follow where the English words led, taking merely a sense of direction from the original.

Most important of all, perhaps, is Ionesco's rhythm. It is this rhythm of language, moulding and moulded by the rhythm of the action, that is for me the greatest unifying force in his art as a dramatist.

These observations on Ionesco's use of language were deduced from the practical problems of translation. It is my hope that an awareness of these problems will send the reader to the original French, of which this is at best only an approximation, and so increase his appreciation of the dramatic skill with which Ionesco handles words.

DONALD WATSON

AMÉDÉE OR HOW TO GET RID OF IT

A COMEDY

AMÉDÉE BUCCINIONI, aged forty-five
MADELEINE, his wife, aged forty-five
(AMÉDÉE II)
(MADELEINE II)
A POSTMAN
FIRST AMERICAN SOLDIER
(SECOND AMERICAN SOLDIER)
MADO, a girl
(THE OWNER of the Bar)
FIRST POLICEMAN
SECOND POLICEMAN
A MAN at the window
A WOMAN at the window

AMÉDÉE OR HOW TO GET RID OF IT

A COMEDY

SCENE: *An unpretentious dining-room, drawing-room and office combined.*
On the right, a door.
On the left, another door.
Backstage centre, a large window with closed shutters; the space between the slats is, however, wide enough to let in sufficient light.

Left centre, a small table strewn with notebooks and pencils. On the right, against the wall, between the window and the right-hand door, a small table, with a telephone switchboard on it, and a chair. Another chair also close to the centre table. An old armchair well down stage. There should be no other furniture in the first act, except a clearly visible clock, with hands that move.

ACT ONE

[*As the curtain rises* AMÉDÉE BUCCINIONI *is walking nervously round and about the furniture, with his head bent and his hands clasped behind his back, thinking hard. He is of middle age, a* petit bourgeois, *preferably bald, with a small greying moustache, wearing spectacles, dressed in a dark jacket and black striped trousers, a butterfly collar and black tie. Every now and again he goes to the centre table, opens a notebook, picks up a pencil and tries to write (he is a playwright); but he has no success, or writes, perhaps, one word which he at once crosses out. It is obvious that he is not at ease: he is also casting occasional glances at the door on the left, which is half open. His anxiety and nervousness are steadily growing. While he is walking round the room, his eyes fixed on the floor, he suddenly bends down and snatches up some-thing from behind the chair.*]

AMÉDÉE: A mushroom! Well, really! If they're going to start growing in the dining-room! [*He straightens up and inspects the mushroom.*] It's the last straw! . . . Poisonous, of course!

[*He puts the mushroom down on a corner of the table and gazes at it sourly; he starts pacing about again, becoming more and more agitated, gesticulating and muttering to himself; he glances more frequently towards the door on the left, goes and writes another word, which he crosses out, then sinks into his armchair. He is worn out.*]

Oh, that Madeleine, that Madeleine! Once she gets into that bedroom, she's there for ever! [*Plaintively*] She must have seen

enough by now! We've both seen enough of him! Oh dear,
oh dear, oh dear!

[*He says no more, he's quite overcome. A pause. From the right,
on the landing, voices can be heard. It is obviously the concierge
and a neighbour talking.*]

THE VOICE OF THE CONCIERGE: So you're back from your holi-
days, Monsieur Victor!

THE NEIGHBOUR'S VOICE: Yes, Madame Coucou. Just back from
the North Pole.

THE VOICE OF THE CONCIERGE: I don't suppose you had it very
warm there.

THE NEIGHBOUR'S VOICE: Oh, the weather wasn't too bad.
But it's true, for someone like you who comes from the
South . . .

THE VOICE OF THE CONCIERGE: I'm no southerner, Monsieur
Victor. My grandmother's midwife came from Toulon, but
my grandmother's always lived in Lille . . .

[*Suddenly, on the word 'Lille', AMÉDÉE, who can stand it no
longer, gets up and moves to the left-hand door, opens it still
wider and calls out.*]

AMÉDÉE: Madeleine, for Heaven's sake, Madeleine, what are you
doing? Haven't you finished yet? Hurry up!

MADELEINE: [*appears. She is the same age as her husband, just as tall
or even slightly taller, a hard-looking, rough-tempered woman;
she has an old shawl over her head and is wearing a wrapper for the
housework; she is rather thin and almost grey. Her husband moves
aside fairly quickly to allow her to pass; she leaves the door still
half open.*] What's the matter with you now? I can't leave you
alone for a second! You needn't think I've been enjoying
myself!

AMÉDÉE: Don't spend all your time in his room, then! It's not
doing you any good! . . . You've seen quite enough of him.
It's too late now.

MADELEINE: I've got to sweep up, haven't I? After all, someone's
got to look after the house. We've no maid and there's no one
to help me. *And* I've got to earn a living for both of us.

AMÉDÉE: I know. I know we haven't a maid. You never stop
  reminding me . . .
MADELEINE: [*setting to work, sweeping or dusting the room*] Naturally, no one's even the right to complain where you're con-
  cerned . . .
AMÉDÉE: Look here, Madeleine, don't be so unfair . . .
MADELEINE: That's right, go on! Now tell me it's my
  fault!
AMÉDÉE: You know perfectly well, my dear, that I'm the first
  to sympathize with you, and what's more I'm the only one;
  I find the whole situation most unsettling, I blame myself,
  but . . . I think, after all, you might . . . well, for instance, you
  take a quarter of an hour to clean out a room this size, and when
  it comes to his room, which is smaller, a couple of hours is
  not long enough . . . you hang about in there, just gazing at
  him . . .
MADELEINE: So now you're timing me! Now I'm supposed to
  make my lord and master a recital of everything I do, account
  for every second of my life. I don't belong to myself any
  more, I'm not myself any more, I'm a slave . . .
AMÉDÉE: Slavery has been abolished, my love . . .
MADELEINE: I'm not your love . . .
AMÉDÉE: Slaves belong to the past . . .
MADELEINE: Well, I'm a modern slave, then!
AMÉDÉE: You don't try to understand. It's just because I'm sorry
  for you that . . .
MADELEINE: I don't want your pity. Hypocrite! Liar!
AMÉDÉE: You see, it's because I'm really sorry for you that I
  won't have . . . oh dear . . . that I'd rather you didn't stay in
  there and watch him. It doesn't do you any good, and it
  doesn't help . . .
MADELEINE: [*indifferently*] Oh, go and shut the door! Well,
  what are you waiting for? There's a draught . . .
AMÉDÉE: All the other doors and windows are shut; how can there
  possibly be a draught?
  [*He goes and shuts the left-hand door, after a brief glance into the*

room which is presumably on the other side; MADELEINE, *who watches him, does not fail to notice.*]

MADELEINE: What do you think you're doing? Now *you're* looking at him! . . . I get blamed if *I* do it . . . *Will* you shut that door! . . .

AMÉDÉE: [*finally closes the door and then comes towards* MADELEINE] I was only looking to see if he'd grown! . . . You'd almost think he had, a little.

MADELEINE: [*sharply*] Not since yesterday . . . or at least not that you'd notice!

AMÉDÉE: It may be all over, you know. Perhaps he's stopped.

MADELEINE: Oh, you and your silly 'look on the bright side'. We know all about *your* forecasts. I'd rather you wrote that play of yours. [*She looks at the table while dusting.*] You don't seem to have made much progress. You're still on the first scene. You'll never finish it!

AMÉDÉE: I shall . . . I've added another speech, anyway. [*He opens the notebook.* MADELEINE *stops working, broom or duster in hand, and listens while he reads:*] The old man says to the old woman: 'It won't do by itself!'

MADELEINE: Is that all?

AMÉDÉE: [*laying the notebook down*] I've no inspiration. With all I have on my conscience . . . the life we're leading . . it's not exactly the right atmosphere . . .

MADELEINE: You've never been short of excuses . . .

AMÉDÉE: I feel so tired, so tired . . . worn out, heavy. I've got indigestion and my tummy's all blown out. I feel sleepy all the time.

MADELEINE: Well, you sleep all day!

AMÉDÉE: That's because I'm sleepy.

MADELEINE: I'm tired, too, dog-tired. And *I* go on working, working, working . . .

AMÉDÉE: I can't stick it. Perhaps it's my liver. I feel I've aged. Of course, I'm not exactly young any more. Still, to feel like this . . .

MADELEINE: Then rest. What's to stop you resting? Sleep at

night and give up dozing during the day. Stop overeating. It's all the result of self-indulgence. You drink too much.

AMÉDÉE: *You've* never seen me drunk.

MADELEINE: More than once!

AMÉDÉE: That's not true.

MADELEINE: You don't need to be drunk all the time to become an alcoholic! . . . It's that little drink before dinner. That's what gradually poisons your whole system! . . .

AMÉDÉE: You know I never touch anything but tomato juice . . .

MADELEINE: Well, then, if you've always been such a sober-sides, if you've nothing seriously wrong with you, if all your faculties are still intact, wake yourself up a bit, get to work, write your masterpiece . . .

AMÉDÉE: I tell you I've no inspiration . . .

MADELEINE: Always the same old story! How do other people manage, I wonder? It's fifteen years since you had any inspiration!

AMÉDÉE: Fifteen years. You're right! [*He points to the left-hand door.*] I've not written more than two speeches since he . . . [*He picks up the notebook and reads:*] The old woman says to the old man, 'Do you think it will do?' and the one I managed to write today, the one I've just read you: The old man replies, 'It won't do by itself.' [*He sits down at his table.*] I simply must get down to it. Write, in the state I'm in! A man should be in a state of elation to do creative work. You'd need to be a hero, a superman, to write in my situation, in such wretched poverty . . .

MADELEINE: Have you ever seen a superman living in poverty? You must be the first!

AMÉDÉE: I must, I *must* get down to it. It's hard, terribly hard, but I simply *must* get down to it! . . .

[*He has collapsed at his table, leaning on his elbows, his head in his hands, staring vacantly, drawn and haggard; then slowly his arm falls along the table with his forehead resting on it. Dumb show. Meanwhile* MADELEINE *has finished her cleaning; when she sees her husband's attitude, she shrugs her shoulders and mutters between her teeth:*]

MADELEINE: [*aside*] Lazy so-and-so!

[*She takes off her apron and her shawl, bundling them up with her broom and duster, and makes for the left-hand door; as she reaches it and half opens it, AMÉDÉE suddenly raises his head.*]

AMÉDÉE: Are you going into his room again! . . .

MADELEINE: [*showing him what she is carrying*] I hope you don't mind if I get rid of all this! Where do you expect me to put it? I can't leave it all in the dining-room! We haven't got dozens of rooms, you know!

AMÉDÉE: No, of course not. But don't stay there too long.

MADELEINE: I couldn't in any case. You know perfectly well I've got to get to work to earn our living . . . And what a living!

[*She goes into the room on the left. AMÉDÉE watches her with a worried look, hesitates, then gets up and moves cautiously towards the left-hand door, which has been left half open; he makes a despondent gesture and suddenly turns to go back to his table, but he is too late, and MADELEINE bumps into him as she comes back.*]

MADELEINE: Look out, can't you? That hurt!

AMÉDÉE: I'm sorry, I didn't do it on purpose! . . .

MADELEINE: It's really too much! . . . Spying on me now!

AMÉDÉE: Is he still growing?

MADELEINE: Shut the door. Were you born in a barn?

[*AMÉDÉE goes to shut the door, but delays a moment to glance into the adjoining room.*]

Shut the door, will you! [*AMÉDÉE pushes the door slowly to, still gazing out until the last possible moment.*] Shut it properly!

[*AMÉDÉE does so; MADELEINE notices the mushroom AMÉDÉE has picked and put down either on a chair or on the corner of the table.*]

Where did you find it?

AMÉDÉE: There, on the floor.

MADELEINE: In the dining-room?

AMÉDÉE: Yes, in the dining-room.

MADELEINE: Why didn't you tell me straightaway? You're always hiding things from me!

AMÉDÉE: I didn't want to upset you . . . You've plenty to worry you as it is.

MADELEINE: [most upset, in a whining voice] I don't know—if they're going to start growing in the dining-room now, what's to become of us? All the extra work, too . . . Pulling them up . . . As though I hadn't enough already! . . . Oh dear, oh dear, oh dear!

AMÉDÉE: Sssh! . . . I'll pull them up for you . . . I'll help you . . .

MADELEINE: Oh, I can never rely on you—besides, it's insanitary.

AMÉDÉE: There's only one . . . Just a tiny little one. Perhaps there won't be any more.

MADELEINE: Optimistic as usual, looking on the bright side! I know where that lands us. There's no point in deluding ourselves, we've got to face facts. That's just how it started in *his* room, too. 'Just a tiny little one', you said, 'not to worry, just a freak, an accident.' And *now* . . .

AMÉDÉE: You've found some more today, in the other room?

MADELEINE: You're always wondering why I spend so long in there! I don't go in there for my health!

AMÉDÉE: No, I never said you did . . . But you don't miss a chance to stand and gape at him; you can't take your eyes off him.

MADELEINE: I pulled up fifty only just now.

AMÉDÉE: You see! We're getting the better of them, there were more yesterday.

MADELEINE: Yesterday there were forty-seven . . . *that* was enough.

AMÉDÉE: [desperately] They're spreading, then, still spreading!

MADELEINE: Everywhere! . . . All over the place . . . In between the floorboards, round the walls, on the ceiling.

AMÉDÉE: [trying to seek comfort] They *are* very tiny. It may have nothing to do with him after all . . . Perhaps it's only the damp . . . It often happens, you know, in flats. And you

never know, they may be good for something: perhaps they
keep spiders away . . .

MADELEINE: I suppose you've often seen mushrooms growing
in flats?

AMÉDÉE: It *does* happen, I promise you. In small provincial
towns, especially. Sometimes in the big ones—Lyons, for
example.

MADELEINE: I have no idea whether mushrooms sprout in flats
in Lyons, but they certainly don't in Paris.

AMÉDÉE: We never go out. We never visit anyone. We've been
living shut up here for fifteen years. Perhaps it's different
now, in Paris too. Or even in the neighbours' flats . . . .Paris
mushrooms! . . . How can you really be sure!

MADELEINE: Don't talk such nonsense! I'm not a child. It's all
because of him. [*With a look and a gesture towards the left-hand
door.*] Only because of him.

AMÉDÉE: [*resigning himself to the truth, his arms hanging loosely,
overcome*] Yes. Of course, you're right. There can't be any
other reason.

MADELEINE: It'll be quite impossible if he makes them grow in
here, too. If he's not satisfied with his own room, we won't
be able to go on living in this place at all! [*Distraught*] And it
wasn't what you'd call cheerful before!

AMÉDÉE: Come on now, Madeleine, pull yourself together! . . .
Perhaps there won't be any more. We'll see. It may be just a
freak, an accident. . . .

MADELEINE: [*raising her head to look at the clock*] Nine o'clock!
It's time. I must go to work, whatever happens, or I shall be
late!

AMÉDÉE: Hurry up, then.

MADELEINE: [*as she puts on her hat*] I shall get into a row. They'll
be starting any moment now . . . [*A buzz from the switchboard.*]
They've started already . . . I'm coming . . . [*More gently to
AMÉDÉE:*] Try and do a little work, too, write something . . .

AMÉDÉE: I'll try, I promise . . .

MADELEINE: [*goes quickly to the switchboard, sits down, picks up her head-phones and passes on the call, while* AMÉDÉE *too goes and sits down at his table with his notebook before him; the clock advances a quarter of an hour. It is 9.15.*] Hallo? Can I help you? The President of the Republic? The President in person or his secretary? . . . Ah, the President . . .

AMÉDÉE: [*at his table, re-reading what he has written*] The old woman to the old man: 'Do you think it will do?'

MADELEINE: [*at the switchboard*] The President of the Republic is on tour, Sir, try again in half-an-hour! . . .

AMÉDÉE: [*at the table*] . . . The old man to the old woman . . .

MADELEINE: [*at the switchboard; it buzzes again*] Hallo, hallo . . .

AMÉDÉE: [*at the table, as before*] . . . The old man to the old woman . . .

MADELEINE: [*as before*] Mr Charles Chaplin, the grocer? I'll put you through. [*Another buzz.*] Hallo, hallo . . .

AMÉDÉE: [*as before*] . . . 'It won't do by itself !' . . .

MADELEINE: [*as before*] No, sir, no. The President can't take a call for another half hour, I've just told you . . .

AMÉDÉE: [*as before*] . . . The old woman to the old man: 'Do you think it will do?' . . .

MADELEINE: [*as before*] A call from the King of the Lebanon . . . [*Another call; she listens in on another line.*] Hold on, please! [*She plugs in.*] Hallo, the Elysée Palace? The Elysée?!

AMÉDÉE: [*as before*] The old man to the old woman . . .

MADELEINE: [*as before*] Yes, of course there's a King of the Lebanon . . . but I tell you he's on the line! . . . Is that the President? There's a call for you, Sir. [*Another line.*] Go ahead, please, it's the President of the Republic . . .

AMÉDÉE: [*as before*] . . . 'No, it won't do by itself.'

MADELEINE: [*as before, taking another call. The clock shows 9.30*] Hallo, I'm putting you through. [*Another call, another line.*] No, Sir, there are no gas chambers left, not since the last war . . . You'd better wait for the next one. . . .

AMÉDÉE: [*still at the table, to* MADELEINE] Madeleine, I can't think of the next line . . .

MADELEINE: [*to* AMÉDÉE] Can't you see I'm busy? . . . [*Buzz*] . . .

Hallo . . . I'm sorry, the firemen are away on Thursdays, it's
their day off, they take the children out for a walk . . . But
I didn't say today was Thursday. [*Another buzz.*] Yes . . .
Hallo . . . I'm putting you through . . .

AMÉDÉE: [*standing up, his hands still on the table*] Oh, how tiring
it is to write . . . I feel worn out! . . .

MADELEINE: [*as before, answering another call*] Yes . . . you wish
to speak to his wife? . . . You don't mind if she takes it from
the bathroom?

[AMÉDÉE *sits down again heavily.* MADELEINE *goes on as
before; answering another call, then another, and so on, while
the clock hands move round to 9.45, and then 10 o'clock.*] . . . I'm
putting you through . . . I'm putting you through . . .

AMÉDÉE: [*with a vacant stare*] . . . the old woman with a
vacant stare . . .

MADELEINE: [*as before*] . . . Hold on, please, I'm putting you
through . . .

AMÉDÉE: [*with a sudden glint in his eyes; he's 'found' it*] . . . 'Oh,
yes; it will do all right!' . . .

MADELEINE: [*as before*] You're through . . .

AMÉDÉE: Madeleine! . . . Would you like me to read you what
I've just written? . . . You can tell me if it's any good! . . .

MADELEINE: [*who has lifted her head-phones slightly to hear what*
AMÉDÉE *is saying*] I haven't time just now! . . . In a minute! . . .
[*Another call.*] Hallo . . . hold on please . . . [*The calls follow in
quick succession; the clock hands sweep on; she says:*] I'm putting
him through . . . I'm putting her through . . . I'm putting
them through . . . Hallo, hallo . . . hallo . . . I'm putting him
through . . . I'm putting her through . . . I'm putting them
through . . . Hallo . . . Hallo! . . .

[AMÉDÉE, *taking advantage of the fact that his wife is fully
occupied at the switchboard, gets up quietly, goes towards the left-
hand door, looks into the room as he stands in the doorway, turns
his head to make sure his wife cannot see what he is doing and then
goes softly into the room, leaving the door half open.* MADELEINE *is
still listening in; another buzz.*] Hallo, yes, can I help you? . . .

No, Madame, no, we're a Republic now. . . . Since 1870,
Madame . . . [*Without leaving her place, to* AMÉDÉE:] Amédée,
why is there a draught? . . . [*Buzz*] Yes, I'll put her through . . .
Amédée, can't you hear me? . . . [*She turns her head and notices
his absence.*] Oh! He's gone into that room again . . . What a
hopeless, obstinate creature . . . [*Just as the clock shows* 10.15,
*she gets up and moves towards the left-hand door, angrily, dragging
her feet.*] Amédée, do you hear? What are you doing? Messing
about in there, instead of writing your play! I'm calling you!
   [*She goes into the room, still leaving the door half open; only
   their voices can be heard; from time to time there is a short buzz
   at the switchboard, not too loud and left unanswered.*]
MADELEINE: [*from the room, in the wings to the left*] You were
   watching him . . .
AMÉDÉE: I couldn't help myself . . .
MADELEINE: It won't do any good, it won't *help*.
AMÉDÉE: Suddenly I began to hope . . . I wondered if . . . I
   thought he might have disappeared. . . .
MADELEINE: Just like that, all by himself! You're out of your
   mind!
AMÉDÉE: The day of miracles is past . . . unfortunately . . .
MADELEINE: Come along now . . . come *along*!
   [MADELEINE *comes out of the left-hand room, dragging* AMÉDÉE
   behind her.]
AMÉDÉE: I feel quite sick! . . . Every time I look at him.
MADELEINE: Don't look, then! What did you go to his room for?
AMÉDÉE: I feel quite sick . . .
MADELEINE: Any excuse to stop writing . . .
AMÉDÉE: He's grown again. Soon, the divan won't be big enough
   for him. His feet are over the end already. I seem to remember
   fifteen years ago he was rather short. And so young. Now he's
   got a great white beard. He's quite imposing with that white
   beard. Twenty and fifteen, that only makes him thirty-five,
   after all. . . . He's not really old . . .
MADELEINE: The dead grow old faster than the living. Everyone
   knows that . . .

[AMÉDÉE, *quite overcome, goes and collapses into the armchair;*
MADELEINE *is in the centre of the stage.*]

AMÉDÉE: Oh! What big nails he's got!

MADELEINE: I can't cut them every day. I've got other things to
do! Last week I threw a whole handful into the dustbin . . .
It's not easy to do either. I'm just a servant, I am, just a drudge,
waiting on everyone.

AMÉDÉE: His toenails have grown right through his shoes . . .

MADELEINE: Then buy him another pair, if you've got money to
burn! What do you expect *me* to do? I'm not giving you any!
We're very poor! You don't seem to realize!

AMÉDÉE: Well, I can't very well give him mine, can I? They're
my only pair. Besides, they'd never fit him . . . Now his
feet have got so large!

[*Buzz*; MADELEINE *goes quickly to the switchboard.*]

MADELEINE: Hallo, yes? Can I help you? . . . [*Meanwhile* AMÉDÉE
*gets up from his armchair, goes once more towards the half-open door
on the left and stares out petrified.*] . . . No, Sir, he's not there . . .
At least, I shouldn't think so.

AMÉDÉE: [*without moving*] The shutters are fastened tight. Yet it's
not dark in his room.

MADELEINE: [*moves up to* AMÉDÉE; *each time she leaves her office,
she takes off her hat; she puts it on again whenever she goes back*]
The light comes from his eyes. You've forgotten to close the
lids again.

AMÉDÉE: His eyes haven't aged. They're still as beautiful. Great
green eyes. Shining like beacons. I'd better go and close them
for him.

MADELEINE: And *you* think they're beautiful! You're talking
like a book. You've plenty of inspiration in real life. Funny
idea of beauty, though.

AMÉDÉE: I didn't say it was funny.

MADELEINE: We could get along without his kind of beauty,
it takes up too much space. [*Slight cracking noises can be heard
coming from the adjoining room.*] Did you hear that?

AMÉDÉE: He's growing. It's quite natural. He's branching out.

MADELEINE: What do you take him for, a tree? He's just making himself at home! Why, he'll soon monopolize the whole place! Where am I going to put him? *You* don't care. *You* don't have to do the housework!

AMÉDÉE: Of course, I know, he gives us a lot of trouble, but in spite of that he's made a great impression on me. When I think . . . ah, it might all have been so different . . .

MADELEINE: Now I suppose you're going to find another excuse to stand there doing nothing . . . Go and write!

AMÉDÉE: All right! . . . All right! . . .

    [*Buzz*]

MADELEINE: [*while* AMÉDÉE *makes for his desk-table*] Never a minute's peace! [*Picking up the head-phones, to* AMÉDÉE:] Shut the door! [*Answering the telephone:*] Hallo, yes, can I help you? . . .

AMÉDÉE: [*returns to the door, puts his hand on the door-knob, looks again into the room, glances at* MADELEINE *busy at the switchboard and seems to hesitate; then he closes the door and returns again to his table to work. He sits down.*] The old man says to the old woman . . .

    [*Another buzz.*]

MADELEINE: [*to* AMÉDÉE, *before answering the telephone*] You still haven't closed the lids! [*At the telephone:*] Yes, Your Worship the Mayor? I'll put you through to the Mayoress.

AMÉDÉE: I'm going . . .

    [*He gets up and goes towards the door on the left; before he reaches it,* MADELEINE *says:*]

MADELEINE: [*to* AMÉDÉE. *The clock should now show* 11.15] You might go and do the shopping, or we shan't have anything for lunch. Take the basket.

AMÉDÉE: [*annoyed*] In such circumstances it's not easy to write. And you're surprised I can't get on with it. Afterwards you'll say it's my fault again. I can't work, I can't work! I don't have the normal conditions necessary for intellectual work . . .

MADELEINE: What have you been dreaming about until now? You always seem to discover the will to work at the last minute.

AMÉDÉE: That's not true! . . .

MADELEINE: *I* can't leave my office *either*. You can see that for yourself. I can't risk losing my job, unless you find some other way of supporting us. You don't think I enjoy this, do you? Of course, if you want us both to starve, it's all the same to me.

AMÉDÉE: And it's all the same to me, too. This life's not worth living!

MADELEINE: I don't know what you'd do, if you didn't get enough to eat. You're always complaining you're ravenous, wanting to stuff yourself all day long . . . [*Buzz*] Do you hear what I say? [*She answers the telephone:*] Can I help you, Madame! [*To* AMÉDÉE:] Hurry up and take the basket or there'll be nothing left at the market!

[AMÉDÉE *makes for the left-hand door and lays his hand on the doorknob.*]

MADELEINE: [*still at the switchboard, watches him*] What are you going into his room for now?

AMÉDÉE: The basket . . . the basket . . . You told me to take the basket!

MADELEINE: That's not where it's kept! You never know where anything is! [*Buzz*] Hallo . . . one moment, please! [*To* AMÉDÉE:] There under the table . . . That's where it's kept. Try not to forget next time. [*On the telephone:*] Number engaged!

AMÉDÉE: [*bends down and sees the basket*] Oh yes! . . . And the rope?

MADELEINE: In the basket. [*On the telephone:*] Yes, Mademoiselle, of course I'll read you the official statement . . . It's a pleasure.

AMÉDÉE: [*picks up the basket and stands up straight*] Oh yes, this is it.

MADELEINE: [*on the telephone*] It is forbidden for trucks weighing more than ten tons . . . You can take it at dictation speed? Very well, Mademoiselle. Yes, I'll read it slowly. No trouble at all . . . Take your time, I'm in no hurry . . .

AMÉDÉE: [*walks very slowly to the rear window, holding the basket, which has a rope tied to the handle; the hands of the clock should now stand at* 11.45] This rope isn't very long. It's a good thing we only live on the first floor.

MADELEINE: [*at the telephone*] It is forbidden for trucks weighing more than ten tons . . . That's right, ten tons . . . to cross the permanent way . . . [AMÉDÉE *gently raises the Venetian blinds, or pushes the shutters a short way and, holding the rope, lowers the basket.*] Amédée, what are you doing? People will see us!

AMÉDÉE: [*his head turned towards* MADELEINE] I've got to lower the basket! . . .

MADELINE: [*at the telephone*] No . . . I was speaking to my husband, I'm so sorry . . . [*To* AMÉDÉE:] Don't buy any sausages, pork upsets you. [*At the telephone:*] . . . to cross the permanent way between midnight and eight o'clock in the morning . . .

AMÉDÉE: [*to* MADELEINE] What must I buy, then?

MADELEINE: [*to* AMÉDÉE] Buy what you like. [*At the telephone:*] . . . without written authority . . .

AMÉDÉE: [*addressing someone presumably down below in the street*] Put in a pound of plums, please! . . . A cream cheese.

MADELEINE: [*at the telephone*] . . . without written authority from the Sanitary Inspector . . .

AMÉDÉE: [*as before*] . . . Two rusks, two pots of yoghourt . . .

MADELEINE: [*at the telephone*] . . . which may be obtained on submission of a written request to Police Headquarters . . .

AMÉDÉE: [*as before*] . . . fifty grammes of table salt . . .

MADELEINE: [*as before*] . . . countersigned by the Chief Constable.

AMÉDÉE: [*as before*] . . . That's all . . . Thank you . . . You can let go.

[*He pulls the basket up by the rope.*]

MADELEINE: [*as before*] Hallo . . . Yes, that's right, Mademoiselle . . . Oh, no . . . You needn't read it back . . . Thanks all the same.

[AMÉDÉE *has pulled the basket in and closed the shutters; he goes and empties the contents of the basket out on the table, next to his notebooks. It is noon by the clock.*]

MADELEINE: Twelve o'clock. [*She lays the head-phones down.*] At last! . . .

[*She takes off her hat and goes towards* AMÉDÉE.]

AMÉDÉE: Have you finished?

MADELEINE: Yes and about time too. I'm exhausted . . . I don't like this brand of cream cheese. You've forgotten the leeks.

AMÉDÉE: You didn't tell me to buy any. [*Nodding his head towards the left-hand door:*] I say, Madeleine, do you think he's forgiven us?

MADELEINE: [*sitting down to table facing the door on the left, while* AMÉDÉE *is still standing facing the same way*] I don't know.

AMÉDÉE: We can't tell.

[*He makes a move towards the door.*]

MADELEINE: Sit down and eat. What are you waiting for?

AMÉDÉE: [*sitting down next to* MADELEINE, *but facing the audience*] He may have forgiven us. I believe he has. [*A long, heavy silence; they are eating their plums.*] Ah, if only we could be sure he'd forgiven us!

[*Another silence.*]

MADELEINE: If he'd forgiven us, he'd have stopped growing. As he's still growing, he must still be feeling spiteful. He still has a grudge against us. The dead are terribly vindictive. The living forget much sooner.

AMÉDÉE: Dash it! They've got their whole lives in front of them! . . . Perhaps he's not as wicked as the others. He wasn't very wicked when he was alive . . .

MADELEINE: That's what you think! They're all alike. Look, I tell you he's growing. He's sowing mushrooms all over the place. If that isn't wickedness!

AMÉDÉE: Perhaps he's not doing it on purpose! He's growing very slowly . . . only a little at a time.

MADELEINE: A bit more every day, every day a bit more, it all adds up . . .

[*Silence*]

AMÉDÉE: Do you mind if I go and look? Perhaps he's stopped.

MADELEINE: I will not have him talked about at table.

AMÉDÉE: Don't upset yourself, Madeleine . . .

MADELEINE: I want to have my lunch in peace. At least, let's have peace and quiet at meal-times. I've worries enough all day. I'm not asking too much, I hope! . . .

AMÉDÉE: No, Madeleine. Just as you like, Madeleine.
  [*They eat in silence.*]
MADELEINE: It's so hot in here. I'm stifling . . .
AMÉDÉE: I hadn't noticed it.
MADELEINE: Open the door, and let's have a little air . . .
AMÉDÉE: Which door?
MADELEINE: [*indicating the left-hand door*] That one. You surely
  weren't thinking of opening the landing door.
AMÉDÉE: You're getting excited again.
MADELEINE: It's not that I want to look at him, I tell you. I'm
  too hot. I want a breath of air, that's all.
AMÉDÉE: Now, listen, Madeleine . . . It's not very wise.
MADELEINE: Please do as I ask.
AMÉDÉE: Very well . . . But I think it's a mistake . . . [*He gets
  up, opens the door and returns to the table.*] It won't make it any
  cooler, you know. There won't be any more air. The windows
  in his room are closed. [MADELEINE *is gazing through the open
  door from where she is sitting; she has stopped eating.*] Aren't you
  hungry? [MADELEINE *does not reply.*] Aren't you hungry?
MADELEINE: Oh, leave me alone, give me a moment to breathe . . .
  [*The eyes of both are fixed on the room. A short silence.*] What
  have I ever done to deserve this . . . to be persecuted like this . . .
AMÉDÉE: It's just the same for me, you know . . .
MADELEINE: No, it's not. You don't feel it so much, you're not
  so sensitive.
AMÉDÉE: Well, I . . .
MADELEINE: I didn't mean it that way. I'm not blaming you.
  You're just luckier than I am.
AMÉDÉE: Luckier than you?
MADELEINE: Of course. At least you can write and think about
  something else, with all your books and literature, you can
  escape from the worry of it . . . whereas I've got nothing . . .
  Nothing but the office and the housework . . .
AMÉDÉE: Poor Madeleine!
MADELEINE: [*annoyed*] I don't need your pity either . . .
  [*A short silence; they look towards the room.*]

AMÉDÉE: You'd almost think he was breathing. [*A short silence.*] What an expressive face he's got! [*Silence*] You'd almost think he could hear us.

MADELEINE: Well, we're not saying anything bad about him! [*Silence*]

AMÉDÉE: He *is* handsome.

MADELEINE: He *was* handsome. He's too old now.

AMÉDÉE: He's *still* handsome! . . . [*Silence*] Has he forgiven us yet? Has he forgiven us? [*Short pause.*] We put him in the best room, *our* bedroom when we were first married . . . [*He tries to take* MADELEINE's *hand, but she withdraws it.*]

MADELEINE: Finish your lunch! Brrr! . . . I feel terribly cold . . .

AMÉDÉE: Would you like me to shut the door?

MADELEINE: [*not listening to him*] Bring me my shawl.

AMÉDÉE: [*rises slowly to his feet, stands and glances for a moment into the room, then goes to look for* MADELEINE's *shawl in some other part of the dining-room, and says*] You'd almost believe he could see us!

MADELEINE: You've forgotten to close the lids again! You see, you never remember! It's always, always left to me!

AMÉDÉE: Yes . . . I'll go and fetch your shawl first, you're cold! . . .

MADELEINE: I'd rather you closed his eyelids! [AMÉDÉE *makes for the left-hand room: steps are heard on the stairs; then a cough.*]

AMÉDÉE: [*stopping within a yard of the bedroom door*] Ssh! Someone's coming.

MADELEINE: Well, who do you think it is? It's one of the neighbours coming home. No one has been to see us for fifteen years! We've lost touch with everybody.

AMÉDÉE: One visit would be enough. [*A voice is heard on the landing.*] Listen! [*Someone can be vaguely heard saying 'Buccinioni'.*] I heard them say our name.

MADELEINE: [*becoming alarmed*] You're imagining things! [*However, the name 'Buccinioni' is heard again, more distinctly this time:* MADELEINE *rises.*] Good Heavens! . . . [*To* AMÉDÉE:] What did I tell you?

[*They both listen breathlessly while the following is heard*:]

THE POSTMAN'S VOICE: [*on the landing*] M. Buccinioni's flat please?

THE VOICE OF THE CONCIERGE: [*on the landing*] It's right opposite. They're sure to be in. They never go out.

[*Noise of a door being shut.*]

MADELEINE: [*to* AMÉDÉE] I told you it was for us . . . Oh dear, oh dear!

AMÉDÉE: [*losing his head*] We mustn't lose our heads . . .

[*A knock is heard on the right.*]

MADELEINE: [*indicating the left-hand door*] For Heaven's sake shut that door!

[AMÉDÉE *hurriedly pushes the door to, while* MADELEINE *dashes over to it and stands with her back to it as though at bay; she is panic-stricken: more knocking at the door on the right. Her hand on her heart*:] Go and see . . . [AMÉDÉE *hesitates.*] Go and see. It doesn't help not to answer. It would only make things worse. It's so easy to break a door in.

[AMÉDÉE *makes for the right-hand door, while the following is heard from the landing*:]

THE VOICE OF THE CONCIERGE: Knock a little louder! They're always at home!

[*Several knocks.*]

MADELEINE: [*without moving, in a whisper*] Open it, go on . . . [AMÉDÉE *moves to do so.*] No, don't . . .

AMÉDÉE: [*to* MADELEINE] It wouldn't do any good. It's so easy to break a door in.

MADELEINE: Have a peep and see who it is, first.

AMÉDÉE: [*to* MADELEINE] Ssh!

[*Then he bends down cautiously and looks through the keyhole, while the following is heard from the landing.*]

THE VOICE OF THE CONCIERGE: Knock louder, they can't have heard you.

[*This makes* MADELEINE *and* AMÉDÉE *jump violently.*]

MADELEINE: [*with a beating heart*] Oh my God! Who on earth can it be? We don't know anybody . . .

AMÉDÉE: [*straightening up, to* MADELEINE] The postman!

THE POSTMAN: [*from outside*] M. Buccinioni! M. Buccinioni!

MADELEINE: [*terrified*] A postman! Impossible! You've made a mistake . . . It's all your fault, you and your old friends, it's all because of your old friends . . .

AMÉDÉE: [*while* MADELEINE *stands there gasping, with outstretched arms, as though ready to forbid anyone to enter the room*] I'm just coming! I'll open the door, why shouldn't I open it? [*He opens the door. The* POSTMAN *comes in.*] You see, you can come in, now I've opened the door, come right in, I've nothing to hide, there's nothing to hide in this flat.

MADELEINE: [*almost clinging to the door-frame*] We've nothing to hide, there's nothing to hide in this flat.

AMÉDÉE: My wife and I were just saying: 'Why shouldn't we open the door?'

THE POSTMAN: [*as though there was nothing unusual*] Perfectly natural, Sir.

MADELEINE: [*without moving, to* AMÉDÉE] Why does he say it's natural? [*To the* POSTMAN:] Why do you say it's natural?

THE POSTMAN: [*still quite indifferent*] A letter for you . . .

AMÉDÉE: Oh no, there can't be.

MADELEINE: Who'd write to us? That's just what I was saying to my husband! Are you really only a postman?

AMÉDÉE: [*to* MADELEINE] Of course he is, Madeleine. What *are* you thinking of?

MADELEINE: [*to the* POSTMAN] Then you can't possibly have a letter for us! Who do you think we are for people to write to us?

THE POSTMAN: Yes, a letter for M. Amédée Buccinioni!

MADELEINE: That's our name! [*She has come slightly away from the door, but returns quickly as soon as she realizes it.*] There's nothing, nobody in this room!

AMÉDÉE: [*taking the letter from the* POSTMAN] Why, yes he's right! It's amazing, but it is for us: Amédée Buccinioni . . .

MADELEINE: How awful!

[*The* POSTMAN *turns to go, while* AMÉDÉE *is examining the letter.*]

AMÉDÉE: Look! It's a mistake, it really is a mistake!

THE POSTMAN: You're not M. Amédée Buccinioni, then?

AMÉDÉE: I'm not the only Amédée Buccinioni in Paris! Nearly half the people in Paris have that name.

[*He holds out the letter to the* POSTMAN, *who takes it back. A prolonged cracking noise comes from the room on the left.* MADELEINE, *horrified, stifles a scream, then utters a peal of laughter to cover the noise.*]

THE POSTMAN: Yet I take it you are M. Amédée Buccinioni of Number 29, Generals Road . . .

AMÉDÉE: There's more than one number 29, Generals Road, there's more than one Generals Road, there are lots of them . . .

[*He casts a worried look at the floor, just by the table, and shows something to* MADELEINE, *who is still motionless*:] . . . Another one, Madeleine! . . . generals sprout like mushrooms . . .

THE POSTMAN: [*poker-faced*] You grow house mushrooms?

AMÉDÉE: [*quickly, to the* POSTMAN] You see, it really is a mistake. I am not Amédée Buccinioni, but A-MÉ-DÉE-BUCCINIONI; I don't live at 29 Generals Road, but at 29 Generals Road . . . You see, the capital A of Amédée on the envelope is written in round hand; my Christian name, Amédée, begins with a Roman capital . . .

MADELEINE: They insisted on calling him after his godfather! You see, it *was* a mistake.

THE POSTMAN: [*examining the letter*] You're right, Monsieur, what you say is correct.

AMÉDÉE: [*to the* POSTMAN] Nobody knows us at all, nobody ever writes to us, I assure you.

THE POSTMAN: Sorry to have troubled you. Sign, please, Monsieur!

[*He presents a notebook.*]

MADELEINE: You're not going to make us sign that, are you? We're respectable people.

THE POSTMAN: Oh, it doesn't matter, Madame. It's optional. So sorry. Good-day to you!

[*He turns to go.*]

MADELEINE: *We're* sorry we can't offer you a glass of wine. We've nothing in the flat; you see, my husband doesn't drink.

AMÉDÉE: [*to the* POSTMAN] It's quite true. I don't drink. It doesn't agree with me.

MADELEINE: We're really very sorry.

THE POSTMAN: That's all right. It's not the custom in Paris. It's only country postmen who get a glass of wine.

[*He leaves.* AMÉDÉE *hurries forward to open the door for him.*]

AMÉDÉE: Good-bye! [*He closes the door, glances for a moment through the keyhole, then straightens up briskly.*] Phew! . . . It wasn't for us after all! Do you think he was annoyed?

MADELEINE: [*coming to the centre of the stage, complaining*] No one ever writes to us! Not a single soul! We haven't a friend left! We broke with everyone, absolutely everyone! We couldn't invite them home.

AMÉDÉE: [*looking about everywhere on the floor for the mushroom*] I could have sworn I saw one just now!

MADELEINE: [*pointing to the room and finishing her sentence*] . . . with *him* here . . .

AMÉDÉE: [*going down on his knees, then getting up again, a mushroom in his hand*] Here it is! I've found it!

MADELEINE: The second one in the dining-room . . . Don't put it on the table, silly, it's not sanitary, and you know they're poisonous. [*A short silence.*] Listen, today I'll let you break your rule. Have a glass of wine, go on, you look so miserable! [*A tremendous crack is suddenly heard from the adjoining room.*] Oh! I'm frightened!

AMÉDÉE: It's only him, Madeleine, don't be afraid!

[*A loud crash of breaking glass from the same direction;* AMÉDÉE *rushes to the door, followed by* MADELEINE.]

MADELEINE: Don't stand there like that! Go and see!

AMÉDÉE: What can have happened now! [*They both disappear through the door, which they leave wide open; coming from the wings, left:*] He's smashed the window! . . . His head's gone right through!

MADELEINE: [*in the wings*] He's growing both ends at once!
What's he up to now! *Do* something, Amédée. The neighbours
will see him! Pull his head in!

AMÉDÉE: [*in the wings*] That's what I *am* doing!

MADELEINE: [*her back framed in the door*] Hurry up! [*A dull thud.*]
Don't drag his head on the floor! You are a clumsy devil!

AMÉDÉE: [*in the wings*] It's not so easy!

MADELEINE: Lift him up. Lay his head on the cushion. Don't
forget to close his eyes!

AMÉDÉE: [*in the wings*] I can't. There's not enough room.

MADELEINE: [*still framed in the doorway*] Well, fold him in two
then, fold him in two, it's easy enough! [AMÉDÉE *can be heard
breathing heavily with the effort.*] No, not like that. [MADELEINE
goes back into the room and can be heard saying:] Let me do it!
[AMÉDÉE'S *back now appears, framed in the doorway. From the
wings*:] That's it. Like this. I have to show you everything!

AMÉDÉE: [*still in the doorway*] I was doing my best . . . You're
never satisfied . . . Are the neighbours looking out of their
windows?

MADELEINE: [*from the wings*] No . . . Come and help me. You
always leave me to do the hardest part by myself.

AMÉDÉE: [*disappears once more into the room; he leaves the door wide
open and can be heard saying*] But I thought you wanted . . .

MADELEINE: [*louder, but still off stage*] Now pull, pull harder!
[*Their efforts are clearly audible; a dull thud.*] Look out! Be
careful! [*More noise.*] Close the shutters properly! It'll be cold
in here now, without the glass!

AMÉDÉE: It's not nearly winter yet.
[AMÉDÉE *and* MADELEINE *reappear.*]

MADELEINE: That's that!

AMÉDÉE: You see, it's all right in the end.

MADELEINE: [*changes her mind as she is about to shut the door*]
Go and close his eyes! You've forgotten again!
[AMÉDÉE *starts walking towards the room.*]
The neighbours must have heard.

AMÉDÉE: [*stopping*] They *may* not have done. [*Short silence.*]

There's not a sound from them! . . . Besides, at this time of
day . . .

MADELEINE: They must have heard something. They're not all
deaf.

AMÉDÉE: Not *all* of them, they couldn't be. But as I say, at this
time of day . . .

MADELEINE: What could we tell them?

AMÉDÉE: We could say it was the postman!

MADELEINE: [*turning her back to the audience and looking towards the
rear window*] It was the postman who did it! It was the
p-o-stman! [*To* AMÉDÉE:] Will they believe us? The postman
must have gone, by now.

AMÉDÉE: All the better. [*Loudly shouting to the rear of the stage:*]
It was the p-o-stman!

MADELEINE: ⎫
                    ⎬ It was the p-o-stman! The p-o-stman!
AMÉDÉE: ⎭

[*They stop shouting, and the echo is heard.*]

ECHO: The p-o-stman! The p-o-stman! P-o-stman! O-o-stman!

AMÉDÉE: [*he and* MADELEINE *both turning to face the audience*]
You see, even the echo's repeating it.

MADELEINE: Perhaps it isn't the echo!

AMÉDÉE: It strengthens our case, anyhow. It's an alibi! . . . Let's
sit down.

MADELEINE: [*sitting down*] Life's really getting impossible.
Where are we to find new window-panes?
[*Suddenly, from the adjoining room, a violent **bang is** heard against
the wall;* AMÉDÉE, *who was about **to sit down**, stands up again,
his gaze riveted on the left of the stage;* MADELEINE *does the
same.*]

MADELEINE: [*uttering a cry*] Ah!

AMÉDÉE: [*distractedly*] Keep calm, keep calm!
[*The left-hand door gradually gives way, as though under steady
pressure.*]

MADELEINE: [*not far from fainting, but still standing, cries out again*]
Ah! Heaven help us!
[*Then* AMÉDÉE *and* MADELEINE, *dumb with terror, watch two*

enormous feet slide slowly in through the open door and advance about eighteen inches on to the stage.]

MADELEINE: Look!

[*This is naturally an anguished cry, yet there should be a certain restraint about it; it should, of course, convey fear, but above all irritation. This is an embarrassing situation, but it should not seem at all unusual, and the actors should play this scene quite naturally. It is a 'nasty blow' of course, an extremely 'nasty blow', but no worse than that.*]

AMÉDÉE: I'm looking. [*He rushes forward, lifts the feet and sets them carefully on a stool or chair.*] Well, that's the limit!

MADELEINE: What's he doing to us now? What does he want!

AMÉDÉE: He's growing faster and faster!

MADELEINE: Do something, can't you!

AMÉDÉE: [*appalled, desperately*] There's nothing to be done, nothing. There's nothing left for us to do, I'm afraid! He's got geometrical progression.

MADELEINE: Geometrical progression!?

AMÉDÉE: [*as before*] Yes . . . the incurable disease of the dead! How could he have caught it here with us!

MADELEINE: [*losing control*] But what's to become of us! Good God, what's to become of us! I told you this would happen . . . I was sure of it . . .

AMÉDÉE: I'll go and fold him up . . .

MADELEINE: You've done that already!

AMÉDÉE: I'll go and roll him up . . .

MADELEINE: That won't stop him getting bigger. He's growing in all directions at once! Where are we going to put him? What are we to do with him? What's to become of us!

[*She buries her head in her hands and weeps.*]

AMÉDÉE: Come on, Madeleine, cheer up!

MADELEINE: Oh no! It's too much, it's more than anyone could stand . . .

AMÉDÉE: [*trying to comfort her*] Everyone has problems, Madeleine.

MADELEINE: [*wringing her hands*] I don't call this living! No, no, it's unbearable.

AMÉDÉE: Think of my parents, for example, they had . . .

MADELEINE: [*in tears, interrupting him*] And now he's going to bring all his mushrooms in here. You've found two already, that was a warning. I should have realized . . .

[*More cracking noises from the adjoining room.*]

AMÉDÉE: [*as before*] Some people are worse off than we are!

MADELEINE: [*sobbing, tears, despair*] You don't understand that it's not natural, it's inhuman, that's what it is, inhuman, completely inhuman! [*She collapses on a chair and sobs, her head in her hands; every now and again she groans:*] It's inhuman, that's what it is, inhuman . . . inhuman . . . inhuman . . .

AMÉDÉE: [*has been standing by impotently all this time, his arms hanging at his sides, now looking at* MADELEINE *and taking a step nearer as though to console her, then giving up and gazing at the dead man as he mops his brow; he says to himself*] What about my plays? I shan't be able to write any now . . . We're finished . . .

[*The feet advance another twelve inches and make* MADELEINE *jump.*]

MADELEINE: Again! [*She buries her face in her hands once more, sobbing and groaning:*] . . . inhuman . . . inhuman . . .

AMÉDÉE: Now I shall never be able to . . . We shan't even be able to breathe in this atmosphere!

MADELEINE: [*still in the same state and muttering to herself*] . . . inhuman . . . inhuman . . . [*Then she changes the refrain with:*] It's an ideal excuse for you to stop work altogether! [*And returns to:*] . . . that's what it is . . . it's inhuman . . .

[*A buzz at the switchboard; she makes a desperate effort to stand up; it is now one o'clock.*]

MADELEINE: Still, it's time for *me* to get back to work again. It's more than I can . . . [*However, she tries to put on her hat and shouts at the switchboard:*] All right, I'm coming . . .

AMÉDÉE: Don't go, Madeleine, not today anyhow, you're too tired, rest a little . . .

MADELEINE: I must go. What do you think we're going to live on? We haven't a penny . . . [*The buzzer goes again, more impatiently.*] Whatever happens, I've got to . . . [*To the switch-*

board:] Yes, yes! All right! . . . [*To* AMÉDÉE:] Other people
don't care . . . they only want to squeeze you till the last drop
of blood . . . they never think you might be at your last . . .
gasp . . .
    [*Buzz*]

AMÉDÉE: We've still got some food in reserve, Madeleine!
Macaroni, mustard, vinegar, celery . . .

MADELEINE: [*collapsing completely*] We shall go a long way on
that . . . I don't care, I can't stand any more, it's too much . . .
[*Taking off the hat she has just clamped on anyhow, she hurls it
away from her and shouts at the switchboard:*] I won't answer. I've
had enough . . . [*The buzzers suddenly stop.*] . . . more than I
can bear . . .

    [*She falls on a chair; her hat is lying somewhere on the floor;
    her head is in her hands again and she is sobbing hopelessly.*]

AMÉDÉE: [*looks at her and then, completely at a loss, picks her hat up
mechanically; he stands there, in the centre of the stage, holding the
hat and staring into space; with some violent cracking noises still
coming from the adjoining room, he walks very slowly to his armchair and sinks down in it, all hunched up; in a very tired voice he
says*] I can't understand how we ever got into such a mess.
It's so unfair . . . And in a case like this . . . no-one to turn to
for help and advice! . . .

                    END OF ACT I

ACT II

*The scene is the same. When the act opens it is three o'clock. In the
right half of the stage there is more furniture than there was before.
It has been brought from the left-hand room, because the dead man has
taken up all the space. It includes a divan bed, near the door, right, and
perhaps an additional armchair, a bedside table, a standing wash-basin,
a mirror, a wardrobe—various bedroom furniture, in fact. These*

objects are all jumbled round the right-hand door, which is blocked up. The left-hand side of the stage is devoid of furniture, except for a few stools, spaced out so that the feet and legs of the dead man may rest on them; the body takes up a great part of this side of the stage. Also on the left-hand side there are a number of giant mushrooms growing at the foot of the walls. Every now and again the dead man's feet jerk forward towards the right, giving AMÉDÉE *and* MADELEINE *a violent shock on each occasion. Every time this happens* AMÉDÉE *measures the fresh ground covered, automatically, as though it were a reflex action.*

As the curtain rises AMÉDÉE *and* MADELEINE *are on the left of the stage. They are barely visible, concealed by the lumber. Neither of them speaks for a moment, then the dead man's feet suddenly slide forward to the right. At once* MADELEINE'S *head appears, only to disappear again a moment later among the furniture.* AMÉDÉE *comes into the open stage.*

MADELEINE: [*making a brief appearance*] You can actually *see* him growing.

AMÉDÉE: [*goes and makes a chalk mark on the floor by the stool on which the dead man's feet are resting, and then carefully measures the distance between the old mark and the new one; when he has done this, he says*] Six inches in twenty minutes. He's growing faster than ever . . . Oh dear oh dear! [*For a moment he gazes at the part of the body that is on the stage, then at the enormous mushrooms.*] They're still getting bigger too! [*A silence.*] If they weren't the poisonous variety, we could eat them, or sell them! Oh! I'm really no good at anything: whatever I try! I can never make a go of it.

MADELEINE: [*emerging from the lumber and combing her hair in front of the mirror*] I've been telling you that for ages . . .

AMÉDÉE: [*with a sigh*] Yes, Madeleine, you're right. Anyone else could manage better than I do. I'm like a helpless child, I'm defenceless. I'm a misfit . . . I wasn't made to live in the twentieth century.

MADELEINE: You should have been born earlier . . . or a darn sight later!

[*Silence. With his hands behind his back, rather round-shouldered, he strolls meditatively round the left-hand part of the stage; then he stops.*]

AMÉDÉE: If only my morale was a little higher. It's being so tired. Yet I don't do anything special . . . [*He starts making for the bed on the right and brushes against the dead man's legs.*] Oh, I'm so sorry . . .

[*He gently re-arranges the legs and glances at* MADELEINE *to see if she has noticed or not; as he sees she is still busy with her hair, he looks a little more relieved; then, after a few more paces, he suddenly stops. He has an idea. He glances again at* MADELEINE, *then towards the open door to the left, then again at* MADELEINE; *once more towards the door. He has made up his mind; he tiptoes quietly towards the next room and has just reached the doorway when:*]

MADELEINE: [*coming right forward into the front of the stage*] Amédée, where are you going? [AMÉDÉE *stands stock still.*] Can't you hear me, Amédée? I want to know where you're going?

AMÉDÉE: Nowhere, nowhere at all . . . where could I be going?

MADELEINE: I'm coming with you.

AMÉDÉE: I can't move an inch without you following me! I'm a free man, aren't I?

MADELEINE: [*annoyed*] Do as you please, my dear, go ahead, go ahead if you like . . . If you always want to be by yourself! . . . If only getting your own way got you somewhere!

AMÉDÉE: [*retracing his steps*] Very well. I'll never go in again, so there! Now are you satisfied?

MADELEINE: [*shrugging her shoulders*] What a nasty temper! You *are* an impossible creature! I need all my patience, with you . . . . you haven't a single saving grace. You can see where it's got us, you can see the mess we're in . . .

AMÉDÉE: Finding fault, always finding fault! When a thing's done, it's done, no use crying over . . .

MADELEINE: It's easy to talk! Just to shake off your responsibilities.

AMÉDÉE: It's not altogether *my* fault . . .

MADELEINE: Well, I like that! Surely you're not suggesting it's mine!

[*She makes for the left-hand room.*]

AMÉDÉE: Where are you going?

MADELEINE: I can't leave him as he is! Someone's got to clean him up, and I can't see you doing it!

AMÉDÉE: Why bother! What's the good!

MADELEINE: [*does not in fact go; the dead man's feet advance again*] He's growing! Growing again! [AMÉDÉE *moves towards the bed.*] What are you doing? You still haven't closed his eyes! You've got a memory like a sieve!

AMÉDÉE: I feel so *tired*!

[*He goes and collapses on the bed.*]

MADELEINE: As usual, when it's time for you to *do* something! . . . Are you going to get rid of him? If you're really so tired, take some medicine, take a tonic . . . take *something*.

AMÉDÉE: They have no effect on me any more. They just make me more tired.

MADELEINE: This is a fine time . . .

AMÉDÉE: I've no strength left, no will-power.

MADELEINE: A fine time to give in! At the critical moment your energy always deserts you and your will-power dwindles away You'll never change, my lad! Will you get rid of him or not?

AMÉDÉE: It'll be all right, it really will, it'll be all right . . . I'm sure it will . . . it's simply got to be all right . . .

MADELEINE: You really believe that, do you? [*Then, suddenly changing her tone:*] It's sheer madness! Do you expect it to put itself right? . . . Something has got to be done, something positive! Now listen to me! If you don't get rid of him, I'm going to get a divorce.

AMÉDÉE: It's not the right time to do that. I couldn't look after him all by myself.

MADELEINE: Do you intend to get rid of him, then? Yes or No? Answer me!

AMÉDÉE: I'm thinking about it, Madeleine. Seriously I am.

MADELEINE: You're thinking! It's ages since you first started thinking about it! If you don't decide what to do, the neighbours are bound to notice something. And soon there won't be enough room for him . . .

AMÉDÉE: As if the neighbours cared . . .

MADELEINE: That's what you think. Listen! . . .

[From the landing can be heard the voice of the CONCIERGE and a man's voice:]

THE VOICE OF THE CONCIERGE: There's something very peculiar going on in this house . . .

THE MAN'S VOICE: Yes, they're a rum lot!

MADELEINE: Did you hear? And it's not the first time I've heard remarks like that . . .

AMÉDÉE: Oh, people say anything. Just gossip, it doesn't lead to anything . . .

MADELEINE: Until they find out and the trouble starts . . . We'll be the talk of the neighbourhood. And it won't stop at that!

AMÉDÉE: All right. I told you I'd get rid of him and I will. I promise.

MADELEINE: When? When? When?

AMÉDÉE: Tomorrow . . . Let me have a little rest first.

MADELEINE: Tomorrow, tomorrow . . . I know your promises, your 'tomorrows' . . . A whole life-time has slipped away between your tomorrows . . . It's not tomorrow, it's this very day that you've got to make up your mind. Understand?

AMÉDÉE: Very well. If you'd rather, I'll get rid of him for you today.

MADELEINE: If only you meant it! [A short silence.] You do intend to get rid of him for both of us, I suppose, and not just for me? You'll do it a little for your own peace of mind, too?

AMÉDÉE: Oh, if I was alone, you know, I'd get used to it somehow.

MADELEINE: But where would you put him? Where would you put him? This is such a tiny flat. We don't live in the Louvre, full of long galleries you could shunt a train in . . . Even if we did, he'd fill them all.

AMÉDÉE: I only need a little space, a tiny little corner to live in . . .

MADELEINE: You call that 'living' . . .

AMÉDÉE: Oh, leave me alone . . . It's just fate.

MADELEINE: You're quite hopeless . . . We haven't much future left, you might at least try and make it a little more pleasant . . . [*To herself:*] What will people say! What *will* people say!

AMÉDÉE: You don't give me a moment's peace . . . Do you think I'm not suffering, too? I'm not the same as I used to be, either. And you say I haven't changed!

MADELEINE: I've been telling you it's all your fault, and I'll go on telling you until I can get it into your thick head.

AMÉDÉE: [*weakly*] No. It's not only *my* fault.

MADELEINE: It is, it is! [AMÉDÉE, *beaten, shrugs his shoulders, says nothing, but simply moves his lips to form the 'Tisn't' of an obstinate child; it is quite inaudible. Silence.*] You ought to have reported his death at the time. Or else got rid of the body sooner, when it was easier. You can't deny that you're lazy, idle, untidy . . .

AMÉDÉE: Dead tired, more than anything, dead tired.

MADELEINE: [*continuing*] You never know where you put your own things. You waste three-quarters of your time looking for them, rummaging about in the drawers. And then I find them for you under the bed, all over the place. You're always taking on jobs you never finish. You make plans, give them up and then let everything slide. If I hadn't been here to keep us both alive . . . with the little I earn . . . and now *that's* gone . . .

[*In his armchair or on the bed,* AMÉDÉE *suffers it all without a word, crushed; his face, turned towards the audience, is expressive of immense fatigue.* MADELEINE, *taking it up again, after a pause:*] You've let fifteen years go by . . . Fifteen years! . . . Now we'll never make anyone believe that nothing's happening here, that nothing's ever happened . . . And it's all because you've no initiative . . . [*The dead man makes another sudden jerk forward.* AMÉDÉE *rises painfully to his feet, like a robot, and goes to measure the latest progress, makes a new chalk mark, returns to his armchair and falls heavily into it, while*

MADELEINE, *with hardly a pause, goes on with her tirade:*] It might be better to tell the police after all, if you won't do anything else . . .

AMÉDÉE: There'd be such a fuss . . .

MADELEINE: Anyway, if we could prove he'd been dead for fifteen years . . . they can't prosecute when a man's been dead for fifteen years . . .

AMÉDÉE: Thirteen . . .

MADELEINE: You see, even thirteen's enough, and in our case it's fifteen . . . If you'd reported his death at the time, we'd be all right now . . . We'd be feeling much safer . . . Not so afraid of the neighbours. This place would be more cheerful and we shouldn't be living like prisoners, like criminals . . . [*She indicates the dead man.*] Because of him, everything goes wrong. . .

AMÉDÉE: I'll never succeed, Madeleine, in teaching you logic. If we'd gone to the authorities the day he died, we'd have been in prison long ago or probably been executed. The fifteen years would never have had time to elapse . . .

MADELEINE: Obviously I must be wrong. According to you I'm always wrong. But I still think . . . Yes, *I'm* always the stupid one, aren't I? That's what you're trying to say?

AMÉDÉE: I didn't mean you were stupid. It's just that you're not logical, which isn't the same thing at all.

MADELEINE: Oh! . . . you and your hair-splitting! . . .

AMÉDÉE: It's no good, we don't understand each other.

MADELEINE: I understand all right. And I've understood you too . . . for a very long time!

AMÉDÉE: I'm sure you have!

MADELEINE: [*after a brief silence*] Or perhaps you could still have gone to the police station the next day, after the murder, and told them you'd killed him in a fit of anger, out of jealousy. After all, it would have been perfectly true. You always said you thought he was my lover . . . And I never denied it . . .

AMÉDÉE: Oh? Is that why I killed him? I'd forgotten . . .

MADELEINE: Scatterbrain! As though anyone could forget a

thing like that! [*Continuing*] . . . And as it was a crime of passion, you wouldn't have had any trouble; they'd have given you some little statement to sign and then let you go free. The statement would have been stuffed into a file, it would all be over and done with . . . the whole affair would have been forgotten ages ago . . .

AMÉDÉE: But as it is, we're still talking about it! . . . Poor young fellow . . . Ah yes! . . . I believe I remember, he had come to pay us a visit. Had I seen him before? Was it the first time he'd come to the flat?

MADELEINE: [*continuing*] tell you we'd never have been in this state, if you hadn't been so careless and always let things slide.

AMÉDÉE: I've always loathed red tape and bureaucracy . . .

MADELEINE: [*still sweeping on*] Whenever I asked you, while there was still time, to go and register his death, you answered as you did just now: 'tomorrow', 'tomorrow', 'tomorrow', 'tomorrow' . . .

AMÉDE: I say, what if I went tomorrow?

MADELEINE: [*forcefully*] No! Today, today, today, today!

AMÉDÉE: Perhaps it's easier to go to the police station . . .

MADELEINE: Yes, easier than keeping your promise. Didn't you just say you were going to *get him out of here today*? Or do you want me to get a divorce?

AMÉDÉE: All right, all right . . . *today* . . .

MADELEINE: Anyway, I can't see *you* going to the police station. Besides, it wouldn't do any good now. Fifteen years after the murder, they'd never believe you did it in anger. If you wait fifteen years, that proves it was premeditated . . .

AMÉDÉE: Look here, Madeleine . . .

MADELEINE: If you're going to tell me again I'm not logical!

AMÉDÉE: I'm not.

MADELEINE: Well, what is it, then?

AMÉDÉE: I'm wondering what we could say to the police . . . As he's grown so old—he does look very old, doesn't he?— perhaps I could say it was my father and I killed him yesterday . . .

MADELEINE: Oh, I don't think that'd be a very bright idea . . .

AMÉDÉE: No, perhaps not. You're right . . .

MADELEINE: Officially, there's nothing we can do now. But we can still get round the law. You've got to act on your own . . . and as quickly as possible . . .

AMÉDÉE: [*gets up slowly and walks round the walls of the room, avoiding the body*] In point of fact, Madeleine, I'm just wondering if I really . . .

MADELEINE: What's the matter now? You're hesitating, aren't you? You don't want to do anything!

AMÉDÉE: Yes I do. I was going to say something else.

MADELEINE: What then? What's puzzling you?

AMÉDÉE: Did I really kill him?

MADELEINE: You don't think it was a poor weak woman . . . like me?

AMÉDÉE: No, no. Of course not.

MADELEINE: Well?

AMÉDÉE: Was it really this young Romeo that we . . . that I killed? It seems to me,—oh, what a memory I've got! . . . it seems to me that the young man had already left . . . when the crime was committed . . .

MADELEINE: You admitted yourself you'd killed him. You said you remembered. You did, didn't you?

AMÉDÉE: Perhaps I was wrong. I may have been mistaken . . . I get everything so mixed up, dreams and real life, memories and imagination . . . Now I don't know where I am.

MADELEINE: If it's not the young man, who else could it possibly have been?

AMÉDÉE: Perhaps it was the baby.

MADELEINE: The baby?

AMÉDÉE: A neighbour once asked us to look after a baby. Do you remember? It was years ago. She never came to take it away . . .

MADELEINE: What nonsense! . . . Why should the baby have died? And why, if it did die, did we keep it here and let it grow up? How careless can you get? And where would you have killed it? . . . Murderer! Baby-killer!

AMÉDÉE: It's possible. I don't know. Perhaps it was crying too loud? Crying babies get on my nerves . . . It must have stopped me working, writing my play. I suppose it must have infuriated me so much, that baby squalling away hour after hour, that I . . . in a fit of justifiable rage . . . a clumsy blow . . . a bit brutal . . . killing babies is as easy as killing flies, you know!

MADELEINE: Whether this old man's really the baby or the young lover doesn't alter the situation. And you've got to get us out of it.

AMÉDÉE: Of course, of course! . . . [*A second later, his face lit up by a glimmering of hope:*] But why shouldn't he have died a natural death anyway? Why do you insist I killed him? A baby's very delicate. It holds to life by a thread.

MADELEINE: It wasn't the baby. My memory's more reliable than yours. It was the young man.

AMÉDÉE: A young lover . . . a lover . . . who comes in . . . drinks a bit too much . . . sees a pretty woman . . . quite voluptuous . . . *that* sends up the blood-pressure . . . a stroke perhaps and . . . good Lord . . .

MADELEINE: So it's all my fault? That's what you mean, isn't it . . . I thought we'd agreed it was nothing to do with me! . . .

AMÉDÉE: I'm sorry.

MADELEINE: To start with, it takes more than *that* to kill a young man of twenty. *He* doesn't suffer from hardening of the arteries, like one old crock I know . . .

[*When she says 'old crock'* MADELEINE *stresses these two words and glances significantly at* AMÉDÉE; *the latter pretends not to understand.*]

AMÉDÉE: Now I come to think of it, I'm not sure it wasn't someone else . . .

MADELEINE: Who then? What are you getting at now?

AMÉDÉE: Listen . . . You know I was in the country one day fishing . . . a woman fell in the water and shouted for help. As I can't swim—and anyway the fish were biting—I stayed

where I was and left her to drown. . . . In that case I'd merely
be charged with not helping someone whose life was in
danger. . . . That's not so serious.

MADELEINE: And how would you explain the presence of this
corpse in our flat?

AMÉDÉE: Oh! . . . I don't know about that. It might have been
brought here for artificial respiration . . . Or it could have
come by itself . . .

MADELEINE: Idiot! You've forgotten it's not the body of a
woman, it's a man's!

AMÉDÉE: That's true. I hadn't thought of that.

MADELEINE: In any case, we'd still be guilty of harbouring a
corpse.

AMÉDÉE: Yes, you're right there . . . quite right . . . [A pause.
He goes on thinking, walking round the walls of the room; he
accidentally bumps into a mushroom, or crushes it; he gives a
start:] I beg your pardon!

    [MADELEINE has seen it coming, too late.]

MADELEINE: [losing her temper] Mind my mushrooms! . . . I
suppose you're going to squash all my mushrooms, now!

AMÉDÉE: I didn't do it on purpose!

MADELEINE: Poor little mushrooms! You've broken all the
crockery already! Now there's not a plate left for you to
practise your clumsiness on . . .

AMÉDÉE: You know, you can't practise clumsiness . . .

MADELEINE: . . . you're having a go at my mushrooms!

AMÉDÉE: There are plenty of them, anyway. Look how they're
springing up, and getting fatter all the time . . .

MADELEINE: You said there'd always be plenty of my plates
too . . . and now there's not one left . . .

AMÉDÉE: Plates don't grow . . .

MADELEINE: No, but they cost money.

AMÉDÉE: Whereas mushrooms, they just germinate and shoot
up . . . At least, as long as *he's* here . . .

    [*He points to the body.*]

MADELEINE: Another reason for leaving him here, I suppose . . .

AMÉDÉE: No, no! Of course not . . .

[*The dead man's feet slide forward suddenly in several successive jerks; they advance a long way towards the right-hand door, very noisily as usual.*]

MADELEINE: [*letting out a distracted cry*] Ah! Amédée! You see! You see! What on earth are you waiting for!

[AMÉDÉE *tries to mark the fresh progress with the chalk, but gives it up when the body jerks forward again; he throws the chalk aside and shrugs his shoulders.*]

What are you waiting for? What are you hoping for? Make up your mind, can't you?

AMÉDÉE: Yes, I see I must. I see I must . . . It's not going to be easy.

MADELEINE: Please, please darling, do something . . .

AMÉDÉE: What did you say?

MADELEINE: [*annoyed again*] I simply said 'Do something', because something has got to be done, that's all. . . . And I said it because it's up to you.

AMÉDÉE: I can't do it straightaway. I must wait till it's dark. Tonight's the time. That's a promise.

MADELEINE: What a relief it will be.

AMÉDÉE You'll be happy at last.

MADELEINE: Happy . . . Happy . . . As if we could make up for all that lost time! All those wasted years, they're a dead weight . . . always with us . . .

AMÉDÉE: It'll be some consolation, anyway.

MADELEINE: I shan't be quite so miserable in my old age, that's all . . .

AMÉDÉE: If you like, perhaps we *could* try and remove him at once . . .

MADELEINE: It's too risky, for both of us. No one must see you. Let's wait till it's dark. What's it matter . . . It should have been done long ago . . . we'll have to wait a little longer, until this evening . . . we've waited for fifteen years . . . what are a few hours more? Oh dear, I'm so used to waiting, waiting, waiting, long uncomfortable years of waiting, that's what my life has been . . .

AMÉDÉE: [*timidly*] So has mine.

MADELEINE: . . . that's what my life has been . . . you could write a book about it! Why have you never thought of writing a novel about my life? Surely, I've earned it. You never think of me!

AMÉDÉE: [*timidly*] I'll try, if you like . . . after we've . . .

[*The dead man advances slightly; from now on the body will advance, slowly but steadily, towards the right-hand door, but without jerking.*]

MADELEINE: If he's still got geometrical progression, will the flat hold him until to-night?

AMÉDÉE: Well, I hope so . . .

[*He makes a rough mental calculation of the distance separating the feet from the right-hand wall.*]

MADELEINE: You might work it out. Then we'd be sure . . .

AMÉDÉE: [*with a tired gesture*] I was never very good at maths. We'll soon see . . .

MADELEINE: You're never sure of anything, are you?

AMÉDÉE: Let's sit down. Keep our strength up. And wait. We can't help it. Can't do anything else. Sit down, Madeleine . . . We've got to make the best of it.

[MADELEINE *and* AMÉDÉE *sit down, he collapsing into his armchair, she nervously on the edge of a chair. Silence. Then, picking up her needles, she starts knitting, impatiently; from time to time she glances at* AMÉDÉE, *then stares at the clock at the back of the stage. The audience should still be able to see its hands, moving slowly at the same speed as the dead man's feet. Meanwhile the room where the two characters are sitting will grow dim as the light through the rear window changes from daylight to a sunset glow, later becoming almost dark in the twilight; right at the end of the act there will be moonlight, coming from a huge, round moon that can be seen through the window.*]

MADELEINE: [*another glance at* AMÉDÉE, *then at the clock. Silence. She is knitting. She looks again at* AMÉDÉE, *who is crumpled in his armchair, facing the audience, with his eyes half-closed; she opens her mouth to say something, then shuts it again. The clock strikes the hour; once more, she looks at* AMÉDÉE *and then*] Amédée!

AMÉDÉE: [*his eyes still closed*] What?! ... Let me get my strength back ...

MADELEINE: You ought to get on with some work ... it'll help you to pass the time until the evening ... Write your play ... It'd be a shame to miss an opportunity like this ...

AMÉDÉE: [*as before*] ... I'm ... so ... tired ...

MADELEINE: Make an effort, Amédée! You know it's for your own good ...

AMÉDÉE: [*as before*] No energy, not up to the mark ... I can't ... no ... really ... not just now ...

MADELEINE: But you've nothing else to do until to-night ...
   [*Silence;* AMÉDÉE *tries to stand up, half rises and falls back into the armchair again. Heavy silence; the body is still imperceptibly lengthening, the hands of the clock are gradually advancing.*]

AMÉDÉE: [*as before*] It's such a long time until to-night. ... I'm scared stiff already ...

MADELEINE: [*less harshly*] Courage, Amédée. Keep calm and you'll forget you're frightened. Control yourself.

AMÉDÉE: [*as before*] I'll try and control myself.

MADELEINE: It's the only way.
   [*Silence*]

AMÉDÉE: [*as before*] It's going to be a tremendous effort to carry him ... it'll take it out of me ...

MADELEINE: Try not to think about it ... think about something else ... forget about it till later ... don't waste your energy. Do a little writing ...

AMÉDÉE: [*as before*] Forget ... when that's all we're waiting for, just waiting for time to pass ... I've got palpitations already ...

MADELEINE: It'll be a nasty moment ... but I'll be there, I'll help you.

AMÉDÉE: [*as before*] The worst part, the worst part of all, I'll have to do myself ...

MADELEINE: Well, it's your turn now.

AMÉDÉE ... and the most dangerous part ...

MADELEINE: It's just as dangerous for both of us ...

AMÉDÉE: [as before] . . . And the physical effort . . .

MADELEINE: You're a man.

AMÉDÉE: [as before] I never went in for sport. I never did any manual labour. I'm no good, even at odd jobs. I've a sedentary occupation, I'm an intellectual . . .

MADELEINE: You never had a proper education or you'd have kept fit . . .

AMÉDÉE: [as before] I realize that now . . . too late, too late . . . But whoever would have dreamt . . . that I should have to . . .

MADELEINE: You have to be ready for everything in life, for any eventuality . . .

AMÉDÉE: [as before] That's true. My parents didn't look ahead . . . No use blaming them now . . .

MADELEINE: [more nervously] And yet at times, usually the wrong times, you do have bursts of energy . . . You managed to kill him all right . . . Pity your strength didn't fail you then, you might have had a bit more to-day!

AMÉDÉE: [as before] Listen, there's no real proof I did kill him. I'm not at all sure I did.

MADELEINE: Off you go again!

AMÉDÉE: [as before] But I told you before!

MADELEINE: Are you crazy or just being awkward?

AMÉDÉE: [as before] I'm willing to admit it, as I can't see any other reasonable explanation . . . I admit it *looks* as if I was the one who killed him . . .

MADELEINE: Well, that's something! . . .

AMÉDÉE: [as before] But it's so easy to find the energy, the sudden strength you need, to kill someone in a fit of spite or anger . . . It just *happens* . . . Anybody could do it . . . It's the prolonged physical effort that frightens me . . . Will it be too much for me? . . . The physical effort, the mere thought of it, the premeditated effort, the waiting, that's what's killing me. [Sighing] I will do it, because I must . . . because I must . . .

MADELEINE: It's all quite simple, then. Try and stop worrying. That'll help. Pretend nothing's the matter. This is a day like any other . . . just as dreary but no drearier . . . Write your

play. That'll put the neighbours off the scent as well. We
mustn't give them the slightest suspicion . . .

AMÉDÉE: [*as before*] No need to worry about the neighbours.
They're not thinking about us. Listen . . . not a sound . . .

MADELEINE: They're there all right. No fear of that. In their
flats, with their ears glued to the walls or the floorboards, or
at their windows, peering out, perhaps, behind the curtains . . .
or downstairs, in silent groups, standing round the concierge . . .

AMÉDÉE: [*as before*] You're exaggerating . . .

MADELEINE: I know them better than you do. It's when they're
quiet I fear them most. People are so cruel, with their callous
curiosity . . . They're always spying on us, they do nothing
else all day. Can't you *feel* them there? Can't you sense how
heavy the silence is? As soon as they've anything to go on,
this uneasy silence you've such faith in will shatter like a vase
into a thousand fragments . . . I'd much rather they were
talking, making sure their nasty remarks are loud enough for
us to hear . . . or even slipping their dirty little notes under the
door . . . or trying to make holes in the wall to put bits of
wire through . . . you know, as they did the other day . . .
I prefer that any time. You know where you stand . . . But
this sinister silence of theirs, I can't get used to it . . . We must
be on our guard . . .

AMÉDÉE: [*as before*] This evening . . . tonight . . . at midnight,
the witching hour, not before . . . like a thief . . . If only we
could get started . . . get it over . . . Oh! If only the time would
pass more quickly! [*Silence*] We've just got to make the best
of it.

[*Silence*]

MADELEINE [*suddenly*] Oh, for goodness' sake do a little work!
How many times have I got to tell you? Don't you realize
we must keep them guessing? . . . As though there was nothing
unusual. . . .

AMÉDÉE: [*still in the same position, laboriously*] Just a day like any
other, any other day . . .

MADELEINE: Oh, write something, do! . . . pull yourself together!

[*Indicating the body*:] Surely *he* ought to inspire you, concentrate
. . . I haven't much heart for work either . . . but I'm going
on with my knitting, as usual . . .

AMÉDÉE: [*as before*] I'll try. I must get down to it, must get down
to it . . . [*Silence*] Why, I believe . . . I believe . . . the images
are rising . . . painfully lifting their heads . . . the words are
taking flight . . . everything's on the move . . . coming slowly
nearer . . . how tired I am! . . . funny sort of job . . . [*With
great scorn*:] A writer . . . [*Short pause.*] I'd rather sleep, until
midnight. But I couldn't anyway . . . no more sleep for me . . .
I—must—write! [*Short pause. Still in the same position.*] The
horizon's a ring of dark mountains . . . Thick clouds are
sweeping over the ground . . . smoke and mist . . . That's it
. . . Come closer, come on, closer . . . [*Still in the same position,
his eyes half shut, he appears to be pulling something very heavy
towards him with an invisible rope; he opens his eyes for a few seconds
and his face should express immense weariness; he does not change
his attitude, he is still crumpled in his armchair facing the audience,
and when he pulls the invisible rope, he does so very slowly. He
is like a man so exhausted and overtaxed that any effort, especially
this, is extremely painful. At the same time he is rocking his head
and shoulders rhythmically from left to right, from right to left, in
the chair; he should look as though, at any moment, his head, which
is swaying backwards and forwards, might snap from his neck and
go rolling into the laps of the people in the first row of the stalls.*]
Come out . . . of the well . . . come out . . . come up . . . that's
right . . . now I can just see their faces . . . im-a-ges . . . im-a-ges
. . . what, what, what are they like . . . there they are . . .
[*While* MADELEINE *goes on knitting in her corner, two figures,
two actors, come in or appear from the back of the stage, and
move round on the same spot during the following scene. They
are made up realistically to look like* AMÉDÉE *and* MADELEINE,
*whose voices they carefully imitate; in the end their voices will
be very shrill, especially that of* MADELEINE II, *plaintive, inhuman, unreal, like the cry of animals in pain. When their
doubles appear,* MADELEINE *will go on knitting where she sits*

and AMÉDÉE *will stay in his armchair or on his bed for a while,
still pulling at his imaginary rope and rhythmically swaying his
head and shoulders, before he finally and gradually becomes
motionless. When he is quite still, his eyes half closed, with a
fixed expression of gloom and weariness on his face, he could, for
example, stay for a moment with his mouth half open. He should
—except for his interruptions and at the end of the scene—appear
as detached as* MADELEINE *from what is happening on the stage.
It should be pointed out that, so far as possible,* MADELEINE II
and AMÉDÉE II *should not be made to look like ectoplasm; to
avoid this, they should not appear in a ghostly glow, but in the
normal lighting for the scene.* MADELEINE II *and* AMÉDÉE II
*should play their parts quite naturally in this unnatural and unreal
situation—just as naturally as* AMÉDÉE *and* MADELEINE *play
theirs.*

*In case of production difficulties, and especially if it is
impossible to find two actors exactly resembling those who are
playing* AMÉDÉE *and* MADELEINE, *this scene can be played as
follows: attention is concentrated on* AMÉDÉE, *so that nothing is
seen but his still face;* MADELEINE *has disappeared; music; the
light intensifies, suggesting a festive occasion.* AMÉDÉE *is a young
bridegroom: he takes from a drawer white gloves, hat, tie, flowers
etc. and dresses.* MADELEINE *appears on the balcony, facing the
audience, as a bride, veiled perhaps. Music.* AMÉDÉE, *looking
very young, moves towards her. If this second possibility is
adopted, there is obviously no need for extra actors: in such case
the dialogue that appears in brackets may also be suppressed.*]

AMÉDÉE II: Madeleine, Madeleine!

MADELEINE II: Don't come near me. Don't touch me. You
sting, sting, sting. You hu-urt me! What do you wa-ant!
Where are you going, going, going?

AMÉDÉE II: Madeleine . . .

MADELEINE II: [*half wailing, half shouting*] Aaaah! Aaah! Aaah!

AMÉDÉE II: Madeleine, wake up, let's pull the curtains, the spring
is dawning . . . Wake up . . . the room is flooded with sunshine . . a glorious light . . . a gentle warmth! . . .

MADELEINE II: . . .night and rain and mud! . . . oh, the cold! . . .
I'm shivering . . . dark . . . dark . . . dark! . . . you're blind,
you're gilding reality! Don't you see that you're *making* it
beautiful?

AMÉDÉE II: It's reality that makes us beautiful.

MADELEINE II: Good God, he's mad! he's mad! My husband's
mad! !

AMÉDÉE II: Look . . . look . . . gaze into your memories, into
the present and the future . . . look around you!

MADELEINE II: I can see nothing . . . It's dark . . . there's nothing
. . . I can see nothing! . . . You're blind!

AMÉDÉE II: No, I can see, I can see . . .

MADELEINE II: No . . . no . . . no . . .

AMÉDÉE II: . . . The green valley where the lilies bloom . . .

MADELEINE II: Mushrooms! . . . mushrooms! . . . mushrooms! . . .
mushrooms! . . .

AMÉDÉE II: Yes, in the green valley . . . they're dancing in a ring,
hand in hand . . .

MADELEINE II: A damp dark valley, a marsh that sucks you down
until you drown . . . help! help! I'm suffocating, help! . . .

AMÉDÉE II: I'm bursting with song . . . la, li, la, li, la, la,
la!

MADELEINE II: Stop singing in that cracked voice . . . It's ear-
splitting!

AMÉDÉE II: La, li, la, li, la, la, la! . . .

MADELEINE II: Stop shrieking . . . stop shri-e-king! . . . your
voice is so piercing! You're deafening me! Hu-urting me!
Don't rend my darkness! S-a-dist! S-a-dist!

AMÉDÉE II: Madeleine, darling . . .

MADELEINE II: Amédée, wretch!

AMÉDÉE II: Madeleine, you used to sing once!

MADELEINE II: Because I was bored, popular songs, only because
I was bored!

AMÉDÉE II: Let's dance! . . . Round and round . . . In a blaze of
joy . . . The light's gone mad . . . Love's gone mad . . . Mad
with happiness . . . Blaze up, joy, blaze up!

MADELLINE II: Don't shoot! . . . Don't shoot! . . . Bayonets and machine-guns . . . Don't shoot, I'm afraid! . . .

AMÉDÉE II: Everyone's embracing.

MADLLEINE II: Don't kill me . . . Have mercy, I implore you . . . don't kill him, don't kill them . . . , have mercy on the children! . . .

AMÉDÉE II: Mad with happiness . . .

MADELEINE II: Madness! Madness! Madness!

AMÉDÉE II: We're floating across a limpid lake. Our boat a bed of flowers . . . rocked along . . . slipping over the waters . . .

MADELEINE: [a cry of terror] I'm sl-i-pping! . . . A boat? What boat? What boat are you talking about? Which boat can you mean? Where can you see any b-o-a-ts! . . . Hee! Hee! Hee! Hee! Boats bogged in the mud, in the desert sand, can it be true?

AMÉDÉE II: White churches! . . . Bells pealing! . . . Churches that are doves! . . .

MADELEINE: Bells! What bells? . . . I can hear nothing! You're deaf, there's nothing, you're deaf . . .

AMÉDÉE II: Children's voices! . . . voices of fountains . . . voices of spring!

MADELEINE II: No, no, they're oaths and toads!

AMÉDÉE II: The voice of the snows on the mountain . . .

MADELEINE II: Forests of slime, nights in the hulks! . . . forests of hell . . . Oh! Leave me alone! Let me go! . . . Aaah! . . . Nightmare! . . .

AMÉDÉE II: The horizon is breathing. Glorious light . . .

MADELEINE II: Where? Where? Beware! Beware! Of the clouds and the wolves! Beware!

AMÉDÉE II: The morning never grows old . . . Sparkling radiance . . . The night is over . . . over . . .

MADELEINE II: I'm sinking into the darkness! Heavy shades of night! . . . Cut them with a knife . . . I won't, I won't . . . I'm frightened! Aaah! . . .

AMÉDÉE II: Madeleine . . .

MADELEINE II: Who makes these brittle leaves grow on the

trees, these stinging branches and clinging creepers?! It's you!
You horrible b-e-ast!

AMÉDÉE II: Madeleine, my own little girl . . .

MADELEINE II: They're lashing my cheeks, my shoulders! It's
you, you devil, it's you who struck me in the face! You
br-u-te!!

AMÉDÉE II: There's nothing in the way. There aren't any trees.
Look carefully . . . Look . . . Stones as soft as moss . . .

MADELEINE II: They blister my feet . . . Thorns of fire! Flames
like needles, flames of ice . . . they're digging red-hot pins into
my flesh. Aaah!

AMÉDÉE II: If only you wished . . . Nature would be so bountiful.
. . . wings on our feet, our limbs like wings . . . our shoulders
wings . . . gravity abolished . . . no more weariness . . .

MADELEINE II: Night . . . always night . . . alone in the
world! . . .

AMÉDÉE II: We are at the gates of the world!

MADELEINE II: [parrot-like] Fancy that! Fancy that! There's no
such thing! Never satisfied! Never satisfied!

AMÉDÉE II: An insubstantial universe . . . Freedom . . . Ethereal
power . . . Balance . . . airy abundance . . . world without
weight . . .

MADELEINE II: Fancy that! Fancy that!

AMÉDÉE II: You could lift the world with one hand . . .

MADELEINE II: Never satisfied! Never satisfied!

AMÉDÉE: [in his armchair] Time is heavy. The world dense. The
years brief. The seconds slow.

MADELEINE II: Stone is just space. Walls are a void. There is
nothing . . . nothing . . .

AMÉDÉE: [in his armchair] It's heavy. Yet it's so badly stuck
together. . . . Nothing but holes . . . the walls are tottering, the
leaden mass subsides!

MADELEINE II: It's going to collapse about our ears! . . . It's
fallen on my head! . . . Oh! . . . those filthy mushrooms, they
stink, they're rotting everything away!

AMÉDÉE II: Every voice echoes ours. Everything corresponds.

We take each other by the hand. There is space, but no distance!

MADE EINE II: I am a widow, I am an orphan, I am poor, sick, old, the oldest orphan in the world!

AMÉDÉE II: Every dawn is a victory! . . . Every sun is rising . . .

MADELEINE II: Never satisfied, wretched man, fancy that, never satisfied . . .

AMÉDÉE: [in his armchair] It's soon going to break right up, into pieces . . .

AMÉDÉE II: Try to remember, remember . . .

MADELEINE II: Don't say that! Don't say that! Never satisfied!

AMÉDÉE II: The sparrows grew strong again in our hands, the flowers never faded.

MADELEINE II: What imagination! What imagination! When? Tell me when? You get on my nerves . . . on my nerves . . . It can't be! . . . not true, never true. . . . All wrong, all wrong!

AMÉDÉE: You are so beautiful, a queen of beauty!

MADELEINE II: A queen of beauty! Fancy that! . . . Who have you mistaken me for, you wretch? He's making fun of me, making fun of my nose! Haven't you noticed my nose?

AMÉDÉE II: You've lost your memory, find it again, find your memory . . .

MADELEINE II: Don't say that. You get on my nerves. Never satisfied. Wretched man. Beautiful, a queen of beauty, fancy that!

AMÉDÉE II: What is far can be near. What is withered can grow green again. What is separated can be reunited. What *is* no longer will *be* again.

MADELEINE II: It's not true! It's not true! Stop saying that. You're breaking my heart!

AMÉDÉE II: We love each other. We are happy. In a house of glass, a house of light . . .

MADELEINE II: He means a house of brass, brass . . .

AMÉDÉE II: House of glass, of light . . .

MADELEINE II: House of brass, house of night!

AMÉDÉE II: Of glass, of light, of glass, of light . . .

MADELEINE II: Of brass, of brass, of night, of brass, of night . . .

AMÉDÉE II: Of glass, glass, glass . . .

MADELEINE II: Brass, night, brass, night, brass, night . . . brass, brass, brass, brass, brass . . .

AMÉDÉE II: [*as though beaten*] Glass, light, glass, light . . . brass, light, brass, night, night, brass . . .

TOGETHER: Brass, night, brass, night, brass, night, brass, night . . .

AMÉDÉE II: The brass and the night, alas . . .

MADELEINE II: Aaah! Aaah! [*Sobbing*] . . . Fire and ice . . . Fire, . . . deep down within me. It's all around me. All about me. inside and out! . . . I'm burning! Help me . . . Alidulée! . . .

AMÉDÉE II: [*together*] Alidulée . . . Alidulée . . . Alidulée! . . . Help, Alidulée! . . . Alidulée . . . Alidulée . . . Alidulée Love . . . Alidulée Love . . . Dear Alidulée . . . Help, Alidulée . . . Alidulée! . . .

> [MADELEINE II *rushes out screaming;* AMÉDÉE II *runs after her shouting:* 'Wait for me! Wait for me!' *The doubles have disappeared.* MADELEINE *rises briskly and addresses* AMÉDÉE *in his armchair.*
>
> *If there are no doubles:* MADELEINE *rushes out screaming.* AMÉDÉE *remains alone. He looks sad. He returns slowly to his table, and takes off his hat and gloves.* AMÉDÉE *has grown old again. The same atmosphere as at the beginning of the second act.* MADELEINE *re-enters from the back of the stage, goes and takes up her knitting and, in a scolding mood, speaks from where she is sitting.*]

AMÉDÉE: [*in the same position as before*] Is it time?

MADELEINE: [*in the same position as before*] No. It's not time yet.

AMÉDÉE: [*as before*] Is it getting near?

MADELEINE: [*as before*] Not really. Patience, a little patience.

AMÉDÉE: [*to* MADELEINE] Poor Madeleine! What a terrible time you've had. [*Looking as though he wishes to approach her:*] Do you know, Madeleine, if we loved each other, if we really loved each other, none of this would be important. [*Clasping his hands:*] Why don't we try to love each other, *please,*

Madeleine? Love puts everything right, you know, it changes life. Do you believe me, can you understand?

MADELEINE: Oh! Leave me alone!

AMÉDÉE: [*stammering*] I know it does! . . . Love makes up for everything.

MADELEINE: Don't talk rubbish! I can't see love getting rid of this dead body. Nor hate either, for that matter. It's got nothing to do with feelings.

AMÉDÉE: I'll get rid of it for you . . .

MADELEINE: It just doesn't make sense! Where does love come into it? Lot of nonsense! Love can't help people get rid of their troubles! You know nothing about real people! When are you going to write an ordinary sort of play?

AMÉDÉE: [*as before*] It's just the way it turns out. After all, I wanted to write a sociological play.

MADELEINE: When you *do* have inspiration, it's always morbid. There's nothing true about it . . . Real life's not like that.

AMÉDÉE: [*as before*] There must be something in the atmosphere . . .

MADELEINE: It doesn't sound like you at all, not like your real self! [*Pointing to the body·*] It's his fault. It all comes from him. *He* must have given you the idea. It's *his* world, not *ours*.

AMÉDÉE: [*as before*] Yes, perhaps you're . . .

MADELEINE: He interferes in everything, don't you realize?

AMÉDÉE: [*as before*] Perhaps.

MADELEINE: There's no doubt about it! [*She slips on the floor.*] It's all slippery . . . The mushrooms are sprouting all over the floor . . . And love won't sweep it clean either . . . [*Glances towards the open door of the room.*] Now we can't even shut the door. He's invaded the whole place! No need to leave his eyes open anyway . . . You still haven't closed them . . .

AMÉDÉE: [*as before*] I'll go and do it . . .

[*He sits quite still.*

In any case he hardly has the time, for suddenly strange music is heard coming from the dead man's room and gradually growing louder; the stage is dark by now and it is eight by the clock. AMÉDÉE *and* MADELEINE *listen in silence and without a move-*

ment in the deepening gloom, which is gradually replaced by a green glow issuing from the bedroom. Other sounds made by the neighbours will be heard while the music is playing: a distant 'Supper's ready!' and the noise of a bell ringing; muffled footsteps on the stairs; the chinking of plates and glasses—it is supper-time; then these sounds slowly fade until only the music is heard. At one moment, just after the music has started, AMÉDÉE gets up and furtively changes the position of a piece of furniture to make room for the body, which is still growing; then he goes and sits down next to MADELEINE amongst the lumber and they both go on listening there, in silence, to the dead man's strange music, both hidden from the audience. In order to reach this position—and to leave it again at the end of the scene—first AMÉDÉE, then AMÉDÉE and MADELEINE, find it difficult to move, as the dead man has been growing and is about to fill up all the available space; later on AMÉDÉE and MADELEINE have to pass between the dead man's feet and the furniture or between his feet and the right-hand door, and this move almost calls for acrobatics. The music should be heard for a long time; stress must be laid on the green light, the jumbled furniture and the stage empty of characters, for AMÉDÉE and MADELEINE are hidden by all the lumber for a considerable period; so, in this scene, what is important is the music, the advancing feet of the dead man and the green light.]

MADELEINE: [*at the very first faint note of music*] What's that? Do you hear? I suppose it's that play of yours again!

AMÉDÉE: No. Keep quiet. It's him, he's singing.

MADELEINE: [*in a lower voice*] But his mouth is shut . . .

AMÉDÉE: [*also in a low voice*] I expect the sounds are coming out of his ears . . . they're the best musical instrument of all . . .

[*The striking of the clock chimes in with the music. Pause. Then the outside noises start up.*]

MADELEINE: [*as before*] It's coming from all directions at once . . .

AMÉDÉE: [*as before*] Each wave of sound gives birth to another . . . it shows how strong he is . . .

[*AMÉDÉE and MADELEINE are silent. For a time there is nothing but the music, then the stage, which is almost completely dark, is suddenly lit by a not unpleasant green light that comes from the dead man's room and first illuminates only one side of the stage.*]

MADELEINE: . . . The light's coming from his room. [*Softly*] That's where it's coming from all right.

AMÉDÉE: [*softly*] It's his eyes shining . . . like two beacons . . . all the better, we don't have to put the lamp on . . . his light is softer.

MADELEINE: Close the shutters.

[AMÉDÉE *goes and closes the shutters very quietly.*]

AMÉDÉE: The neighbours will have finished their supper soon. They'll be going to bed.

MADELEINE: [*still in a low voice, while* AMÉDÉE *comes back to her side in silence*] Well, I must admit he's not without talent.

[*A long pause; a long spell of music; the hands of the clock stand out against the dark background; moonlight steals through the slats in the shutters. Then suddenly, without a word,* AMÉDÉE *and* MADELEINE *rise simultaneously to their feet, a good few moments after the last note of music has sounded.*]

MADELEINE: We ought to move the wardrobe.

AMÉDÉE: Oh dear! He'll soon reach the door.

MADELEINE: You don't want him to go through it, do you?

[*Distracted, but silent,* AMÉDÉE *and* MADELEINE *carry out a series of wordless movements, while the hands of the clock go round faster. They shift the wardrobe in silence; their movements are wild and unsystematic; they change the position of other pieces of furniture, clambering with difficulty from one side of the dead man's legs to the other. In their frenzy it is, however,* AMÉDÉE *who is the calmer or more deliberate of the two. Then* MADELEINE *polishes the dead man's shoes with a duster.* AMÉDÉE *brushes the trousers down with his hand and then adjusts the position of the feet on a stool.* MADELEINE *puts back into the wardrobe she has just moved the duster she had taken out to polish the shoes. At a certain moment, while there is no change in* MADELEINE'S *agitation,* AMÉDÉE *stands still, his back to the audience, his hands clasped behind his back and gazes at the dead man's feet; then his glance slowly wanders the whole length of the body to rest for a moment*

*on the open door. He turns round again, sighing and shaking his
head. For a brief space* MADELEINE *looks at* AMÉDÉE *without
speaking; she seems quite cast down and makes a gesture in his
direction as if to say: 'You see what we've come to now'. Then a
fresh burst of activity, as both characters move haphazardly about
the stage, this time empty-handed. This silent, aimless scurrying
is sharply interrupted by the violent sound of a gong: the dead
man's feet have reached the door. The actor's movements become
slower at once, visibly so, and are once more heavy and dragging.]*

MADELEINE: [*at the sound of the gong*] He's reached the door. It's
time. Are you still as tired?

AMÉDÉE: Have I time to collect my strength?

[*He is standing motionless opposite the left-hand door.*]

MADELEINE: It would have been more sensible of you to rest,
instead of dashing about like that.

AMÉDÉE: It's a long time since rest did me any good. Or even
sleep. When I get up I'm more exhausted than when I went
to bed . . . To think I once had so much vim and vigour!

MADELEINE: You're dreaming again. Vim and vigour! You!

AMÉDÉE: [*in the same attitude*] Oh yes, me . . . It's not fair to say
that . . . I used to bend iron bars with my bare hands and lift
carts with my shoulders. Nowadays, even a feather weighs a
ton . . .

MADELEINE: To hear you talk, you'd think I'd married Mr
Universe . . .

[*The clock shows a quarter to midnight.*]

AMÉDÉE: Has the time really come . . .?

MADELEINE: Yes, it has . . .

AMÉDÉE: [*walks heavily to the window, while* MADELEINE *watches
him*] So the moment's come at last!

MADELEINE: You've still got a minute or two.

AMÉDÉE: [*looking through the slats in the shutters*] Now there's not
a soul in sight.

MADELEINE: Don't look. Someone might see you.

AMÉDÉE: [*looking at the dead man's feet*] His feet are right against the
door.

MADELEINE: So long as they don't go through. It leads on to the
landing. We'd be done for . . . Mind that armchair . . .
  [AMÉDÉE *and* MADELEINE *move the armchair; they push the
  feet sideways a little, to the right or the left.*]
A little more . . . Push. [AMÉDÉE *does so.*] That'll do . . .
There! . . .

AMÉDÉE: Do you think it'll really do any good to get rid of
him? What if another guest turns up, and the whole thing
starts all over again? . . .

MADELEINE: He'd be smaller, anyway. He wouldn't take up all
the room, not at first. We'd have time to breathe before he
grew.

AMÉDÉE: That's true . . . A few years of comparative peace; that'd
be something . . . [*Gazing towards the room:*] He looks older
than he did just now . . . [*He is still standing face to the room, while*
MADELEINE *has collapsed into the armchair. Pause.*] He's still good-
looking, though. [*Pause*] It's funny how, in spite of everything, I'd got used to him.

MADELEINE: So had I . . . But that's no reason for keeping him
here. Look at the clock. The moment's arrived. Now's the
time.

AMÉDÉE: [*from the same spot*] I know. Once a thing's settled, it's
settled. I'm not going back on my word. But I must say that
the thought of saying good bye to him . . . Yes . . . I'll be quite
sorry to see him go . . . [*He walks a few steps and gently pushes
a pedestal table out of the way, to make room for the feet.*] This
door's a good bit stronger than the other one, anyhow.
[*Walking round the stage, hands clasped behind hunched shoulders.*]
If he'd behaved properly, we might have kept him. After all,
he's grown up and grown old with us in this house. That
counts for something! You can't help it, you get attached to
things, human beings are like that . . . Yes, you can get attached
to almost anything . . . to a dog, a cat, a box, a child . . .
especially to him, there was every reason . . . What memories
he brings back . . . Our home will seem quite empty when he's
gone . . . He's been the silent witness of our whole past, which

hasn't always been so pleasant, I admit . . . you might almost say: *because* of him . . . but then life is never very cheerful . . . if it's not one thing, it's another. What I mean is . . . Perhaps we didn't know how to cope with the situation, we ought to have taken it more philosophically. All this might have turned out differently, not much better, of course, but we ought to have tried to accept things . . . We never tried everything, never did all we could to make him feel at home . . . We've all behaved badly at some time or other, so we ought to be more tolerant . . . Otherwise, otherwise, life is impossible. . . . We can't be expected to understand everything . . . so we ought to be more broad-minded . . .

MADELEINE: You're not hesitating again at the last moment. You're not going to back out.

AMÉDÉE: [*with a sigh*] There's no other way. [*Another gong-like blow against the door; the clock strikes midnight.*] You see?
    [*He looks very weary.*]

MADELEINE: You wait. You'll feel better, afterwards.

AMÉDÉE: You think so?

MADELEINE: Quick! Open the shutters!

AMÉDÉE: But they'll see us . . .
    [*Complete silence just at this moment.*]

MADELEINE: Do as I tell you . . . [AMÉDÉE *makes for the rear window and starts opening the shutters; he moves like a robot.*] No one will see or hear you. There's a full moon . . .

AMÉDÉE: [*who has one shutter wide open*] I can't believe this . . . is me any more.

MADELEINE: The full moon blinds them all, dulls their brains and sends them off into a deep sleep. They're all locked in their dreams.

AMÉDÉE: Think carefully, Madeleine, what you're making me do. Think now! There'll be no turning back. We shall never, never see him again. You won't have any regrets or blame me for it, you won't start crying?
    [AMÉDÉE *has opened the shutters wide; the cold light of the moon enters the room, merges with the green glow or even quells it.*]

MADELEINE: This is the ideal time. It's now or never; let's start.
AMÉDÉE: [*gazing out of the window*] How beautiful the night is!
MADELEINE: It's past midnight.

[*The cold and brilliant light is now flooding in through the window. The glowing sky can be seen outside exactly as* AMÉDÉE *describes it in his next speech. There is a striking contrast between the sinister room and the dazzling light effects. The mushrooms, which have not stopped growing and are now enormous, have silvery glints. The varied play of light seems to come not only from the window, but from all sides: through the walls and the cracks in the cupboard from the furniture and the mushrooms, big and small—the young ones sprouting on the floor are shining like glow-worms. The producer, the set-designer and the lighting specialist should remember that although the atmosphere of the married couple's room has evidently changed slightly, it must definitely suggest the mingled presence of horror and beauty at the same time.*]

AMÉDÉE: Look, Madeleine . . . all the acacia trees are aglow. Their blossoms are bursting open and shooting up to the sky. The full-blown moon is flooding the Heavens with light, a *living* planet. The Milky Way is like creamy fire. Honeycombs, countless galaxies, comets' tails, celestial ribbons, rivers of molten silver, and brooks, lakes and oceans of palpable light . . . [*He turns towards* MADELEINE, *his hands outstretched*:] . . . There's some on my hand. Look, it's like velvet or lace . . . [*Meanwhile* MADELEINE *is making the final preparations in the room; she is moving things about, an odd piece of furniture, making more room, trying in vain, and quickly giving up the attempt, to bend the dead man's legs a little.*] . . . Light is silky . . . I'd never touched it before . . . [*He looks through the window again.*] Sheaves of blossoming snow, trees in the sky, gardens and meadows . . . domes and cupolas . . . columns and temples . . . [*Indicating the dead man regretfully*:] He won't be able to see all this. [*At the window again:*] And space, space, infinite space!

[*It is essential that all this should be said quite naturally, without exaggeration.*]

MADELEINE: Don't waste time. What's the matter with you?
The night air's coming in. We shall both catch cold. Let's get
started.

AMÉDÉE: But it's summer-time, Madeleine!

MADELEINE: [*beginning to get excited*] Is there anybody in the
street?

AMÉDÉE: Nobody. Nothing stirring. Not a sound. It's deserted.
[*To the dead man:*] . . . Poor old thing! . . .

MADELEINE: [*as the moment for carrying out their decision approaches
and during the actual operation, MADELEINE gradually loses her
calm and her self-control; it is AMÉDÉE, at the beginning and throughout, who remains, if not calm, at least detached from the proceedings,
acting like a robot*] This is hardly the time to feel sorry for
him! [*What follows is accompanied by growing agitation on
MADELEINE's part.*] Come on, give me a hand, come al-o-ng!
[*AMÉDÉE leaves the window and walks towards MADELEINE.*]
Ssh! Listen! . . . No, it's nothing. Come on, quickly!

AMÉDÉE: They can't see me, you said they were blinded by the
moonlight . . .
[*They are standing by the dead man; AMÉDÉE lifts his feet, then
lets them fall back on the stool; he hardly knows where to begin.*]

MADELEINE: [*almost wringing her hands*] I know I did . . . but you
never can tell . . . I only hope . . . Come on, quickly . . . [*The
intense activity of the following scenes can only be called feverish.
MADELEINE looks at the clock, tries to move some furniture and
gives up; she shows all the signs of acute anxiety.*] Where are
you going to dispose of the body?

AMÉDÉE: In the river, of course. Where else?

MADELEINE: Yes, in the river. [*Her hands pressed to her heart:*]
Have you any idea where?
[*It sounds as if someone is knocking at the right-hand door.*]

AMÉDÉE: [*not frightened, because he is past fear*] Someone's knocking.

MADELEINE: [*hands still on her heart*] No. It's the beating of my
heart . . .

AMÉDÉE: If there really was someone knocking at the door, at

this very moment it wouldn't be easy to tell the difference
... Still, I don't suppose anyone will come ...

[*The music could perhaps start again now. Strong regular beats—*
MADELEINE's *heart-beats seem to shake the whole set.* AMÉDÉE
*is trying to drag the dead man by the feet: it looks remarkably
difficult.* MADELEINE *helps him or tries to make more room by
aimlessly pushing the furniture about. He interrupts his efforts to
speak:*] The most dangerous part, of course, is getting him
from here to the river ... still, it's only five hundred yards
away. The first three hundred are the worst. Along our own
street. The houses are tall on both sides. But ... if I can move
fast enough, while the moon's still casting its spell on the
neighbours, I shan't be seen. Unless something awful happens
and a piercing scream shatters their dreams and wakes them
all up. Never mind! Nothing venture, nothing win. There's
no alternative! [MADELEINE *listens, growing steadily more
frantic.*] I've no choice.

MADELEINE: [*helping* AMÉDÉE *to pull the feet*] Come on, then,
hurry up ... hurry up ...

AMÉDÉE: I'm doing my best! Stop nagging!

MADELEINE: I'm trying to help you, and you say I'm nagging!
I'd like to know what you'd say if I left you to it!

[*In point of fact, each time* AMÉDÉE *manages to raise the feet a
little and drag them, with much difficulty, a fraction nearer the
window—twisting them round to avoid the right-hand door—*
MADELEINE *impedes his progress, complicating his task, getting
in his way and bringing his efforts to nought;* AMÉDÉE *is practically
dragging* MADELEINE *along with the dead body; he has become
amazingly calm, a 'calm robot'.*]

MADELEINE: Pull harder ...

[AMÉDÉE *makes a supreme, a superhuman effort. He pulls very
hard: once, twice, a third time, and then, suddenly, the body yields
to him, with a tremendous crash that breaks the silence, as chairs
are pulled over, plaster falls from the ceiling, clouds of dust rise
and the whole set trembles. This should give the impression that
as the body—its head still invisible—is steadily pulled nearer the*

window, it is dragging the whole house with it and tugging at the
entrails of the two principal characters.]

MADELEINE: [*shouting through the din*] Be careful, or he'll have all
the china down . . .

AMÉDÉE: [*the same and still pulling*] He'd really got rooted in the
flat . . . He's so heavy . . . The strength of inertia!

MADELEINE: [*as before*] His head's not out of his room yet! Nor is
his chest! Shall I go and pull him by the hair?

AMÉDÉE: [*as before*] Don't bother! . . . He's coming . . . [*The noise
is reduced.*] He's coming . . .

MADELEINE: That's it . . . Keep it up . . . Hurry up . . . The time's
going . . . Pull . . . Tear him out . . .

AMÉDÉE [*backing towards the window, still pulling with all his might*]
He's harder to pull out than an old wisdom tooth . . . tougher
than an oak . . .

MADELEINE: Wait. I'll come and help you. [*Help that hinders,
that is pointless and confused.*] Oh, he's heavier than an oak . . .
an oak made of iron with roots of lead . . .

AMÉDÉE: [*has reached the rear window; he lays the feet on the window-
ledge and stops to take breath and wipe his brow*] Phew!

MADELEINE: Phew!

AMÉDÉE: And it's not over, yet. But we'll make it!

MADELEINE: It's specially important to be careful now. You're
wet through already. So long as you don't catch cold . . .
[AMÉDÉE *prepares to resume his efforts.*] Wait a moment. I'll
have a look. [*She stands in the window beside the feet and looks
down the street.*] The street's still empty. We must watch out. I
can't see any police on their beat.

AMÉDÉE: The streets *are* empty at this time of night.

MADELEINE: You mustn't throw him in the water where there
are any barges; the moon doesn't affect bargees. Don't choose
a place like that . . .

AMÉDÉE: [*pointing through the window*] I'll go a hundred yards
farther up. It only means a little extra effort. Whatever I do,
I can't help crossing little Torco Square, there, at the end of the
street.

MADELEINE: [*still looking through the window in the same direction*]
Can't you go another way? . . . That's a nuisance . . . right at
the end there are lights in some of the windows . . . You might
be spotted.

AMÉDÉE: That's the bar and brothel kept by the owner of our
flat. It's used by American soldiers. You can see them sometimes walking about with their girls. There's not much risk.
They don't know a word of the language . . . most of them! . . .

MADELEINE: Try and avoid them.

AMÉDÉE: That's not very easy. I'll have to chance it. It's a lovely
night.

MADELEINE: [*still looking through the window, her back to the audience;*
AMÉDÉE *starts pulling the legs round in the middle of the stage;*
then goes back to the window] Amédée . . . I'm frightened . . .
Oh dear . . . I suppose we must . . . We must . . . You'd better
get on with it . . .

> [*Standing at the window,* AMÉDÉE *pulls the body; it is obviously*
> *going much more easily; the clock strikes; the feet are over the*
> *window-sill and hang down the other side.*]

AMÉDÉE: He's rolling out, now . . . It's a lot easier . . . rolling out!
[AMÉDÉE *is pulling at his legs, and the long, long body, is winding*
out of the room, interminably; at each pull he rests it on the
window-sill, while the long legs go sliding down, presumably
to the pavement, and still issue, of course, incredibly long, slowly
from the other room; the trunk has not appeared yet.]

MADELEINE: [*incoherently*] I'm frightened . . . We shouldn't have
made up our minds so quickly . . . We couldn't do anything
else . . . We should have waited . . . No, we shouldn't have
waited . . . It's all your fault . . . No, it's not your fault, I was
right all the same, we simply had to . . . [AMÉDÉE *goes on*
pulling; the body passes steadily over the window-sill.] Faster,
pull faster, Amédée, I feel sick . . . You're killing me, Amédée,
pull faster, there's no end to it, pull faster . . . [*A loud noise*
comes from outside, from below; AMÉDÉE *stops*] Oh! . . . Amédée,
I told you to be careful . . . You seem to be doing it on
purpose . . .

AMÉDÉE: [*worried, all the same*] What's happened?

MADELEINE: His feet, his feet! They've hit the pavement . . . You should do it more gently . . .

[AMÉDÉE *looks out of the window, too, next to* MADELEINE.]

AMÉDÉE: I'm going down . . . Keep a good look-out . . .

MADELEINE: Am I to stay here all alone? . . . I'm frightened . . .

AMÉDÉE: [*with one leg over the window-sill*] What else can we do? It won't be for long. A few minutes and I'll be back!

[*He climbs out of the window; first only his head is visible, then his hands; finally he goes out of sight;* MADELEINE *watches him climb down.*]

MADELEINE: Be careful, dear, don't take risks, put your foot there . . . there . . . that's right . . . And now there . . . that's the way . . .

AMÉDÉE: [*from below*] All right . . .

MADELEINE: Are you down? Don't make too much noise.

AMÉDÉE: [*from below*] Can you see anyone?

MADELEINE: [*through the window to* AMÉDÉE] Can you see anyone?

AMÉDÉE: [*from below*] I can't see anyone.

MADELEINE: [*through the window, to* AMÉDÉE] Well, off you go, then . . . Don't waste your time! . . . Hurry up . . . Pull . . . Pull . . . [AMÉDÉE *pulls from the pavement below . . . The same thing happens as previously, the rest of the legs appear, passing through the room and out of the window. These legs are surprisingly long, so it should last quite a long time; some strange muffled music could perhaps accompany this action. Meanwhile* MADELEINE *goes on encouraging her husband from the window:*] Pull . . . that's it . . . again . . . again . . . pull . . . there's still some more to come, pull . . . pull . . .

[*At last the trunk appears, and the enormous hands.*]

AMÉDÉE: [*still in the street, pulling, he must have gone some distance already, almost as far as little Torco Square perhaps, with its bar and its brothel; his voice sounds a long way off*] I've got to the square, Torco-o-o!

MADELEINE: [*who has been gazing directly down at the pavement, has gradually raised her head and is now looking farther off*] No.

No-o-o! . . . Go on pulling, there's more to come . . . It's not
finished yet . . . Have you met a-anybo-ody?

AMÉDÉE: No-o-o-body! Don't be afraid! And you, have you?
Can you see anyone?

MADELEINE: No-o-one! Go on, pull . . . pull . . . pull! . . . [*She
is still at the window, with her back to the audience; the body is still
sliding out. Finally the shoulders appear, and then the head, which
is so large that there is hardly room for it to pass through the doorway
on the left; tremendously long white hair, an enormous white beard.
When the head reaches the window, the long hair is still not quite out
of the room.*] Pull, Amédée . . . pull . . . Amé-é-edée . . . pul-l-l
. . . pull . . . pull . . . Watch out for the barges . . . Hurry up . . .
Don't catch cold . . . Go straight there, don't hang abo-o-out
. . . [*The head is right near the window; it should almost hide*
MADELEINE.] . . . Pul-l-l. . . . Pul-l-l! . . .

CURTAIN

ACT III

SCENE: *Little Torco Square. A few steps at the back, a small door and
one or two lighted windows, perhaps. This is the brothel-bar frequented
by American soldiers. There is an indistinct hum coming from it; a
jazz orchestra and men's and women's voices, but the sound should
appear to come from farther off. The shadow of figures dancing could
be seen behind the curtains, but not too much insistence should be laid
on this; the shadows should pass once, rapidly, a fleeting vision. The
music and the noise from the bar, which are only just audible in the
theatre, will suddenly blare forth out of all proportion when, at a given
moment, the door of the bar opens and an* AMERICAN SOLDIER *is
violently shoved outside; then the noise will fade again. Above the
door and the window of the place there is a sign, which reads:* 'BAR-
MAISON DE TOLERANCE'. *Near the steps, there might also be a lamp-
post, between the door and the window. Above all no attempt should*

be made to make the set look like the traditional street-corner of low
repute; it should not look like a tavern or a night-club; the walls of this
brothel-bar are light in colour, it appears quite ordinary and respectable;
the façade is fairly low; then a stretch of wall, which must not be too
high to allow for the stage effect that is to come; the steps could be
situated at one side of the bar-door, so that the latter is on a level with
the stage; the houses to left and right are, on the other hand, tall and
many-storeyed, with numerous windows. Above the wall of the brothel,
an enormous moon, which lights the stage brilliantly. The entrance of
AMÉDÉE *will act as a signal for the light to intensify still further: huge*
clusters of stars will come into view, comets and shooting stars, fire-
works in the sky.]

[*As the curtain rises on the third act the stage remains empty for a*
while. Music and muffled sounds from the bar. The windows of the
other houses are dark and shuttered tight. Suddenly the bar door
is opened noisily; the music and the bar noises are incredibly loud
while the door remains open, they might even come from several
parts of the auditorium; a tall AMERICAN SOLDIER *is being pushed*
vigorously by the shoulders out of the bar. From inside the bar can
be heard:]

VOICE OF THE OWNER OF THE BAR: No drunks in here! Get out!
[*Then the door slams behind the* AMERICAN SOLDIER *the noise*
fades; the SOLDIER *turns and bangs on the door.*]

SOLDIER: No! No! [*Banging on the door.*] No . . . I'm not drunk . . .
Open the door . . . I paid for it . . . [*Renewed banging.*] Open the
door . . . I wanna come in . . .
[*He knocks again. The door opens, and with a strong push the*
SOLDIER *manages to force his way partly back; half in, half out,*
he appears to be fighting.]
No! No! [*Then, yielding to superior force, he is almost completely*
outside again, except for one foot, which prevents the door from
being shut tight.] I'm not drunk! I want some brandy! Cognac!

OWNER'S VOICE: [*from within*] Clear out! Don't you understand!

SOLDIER: [*obstinately*] I paid for it . . . I paid for it . . . I wan'
Mado . . .

VOICE: Which Mado?

SOLDIER: I paid for it . . . I paid . . . for . . . Mado!

VOICE: Mado's a nice girl. She never goes with drunks. Mado . . . not for drunk men.

SOLDIER: I'm not . . . I'm not . . . I wan' . . . I . . . wan' . . . Mado!

[*A violent push from within sends the* SOLDIER *sprawling on the ground; the door closes.*]

SOLDIER: [*sitting on the ground facing the bar and beating his fists rhythmically on the floor of the stage*] Mado! Mado! Cognac! Mado! Cognac! Mado! Mado! Cognac!

[*The bar door opens; the man's voice is heard:*]

VOICE: Shut your blasted trap or I'll call a policeman! A mil-it-ary pol-ice-man . . .

[*The door closes.*]

SOLDIER: [*who has risen to his feet and hurled himself at the door— too late, the door shutting in his face—beats on it with his fists and shouts*] Policeman!? Military Policeman!? . . . [*Then*] I am a Military Policeman! [*He turns and faces the audience, takes an armband bearing the letters M.P. from his pocket, fixes it on his arm and says in a woe-begone voice with his strong American accent:*] Military Police, that's me! [*He shrugs his shoulders, makes a movement towards the door, hesitates, gives it up and says, in a puzzled and disappointed tone:*] Mado! Mado! [*Then, after scratching his head, he angrily rips off his M.P.'s armband, hurls it to the ground, takes a piece of chewing-gum from his pocket and repeats, while he is chewing, in the same woe-begone voice:*] Mado! Mado!

[*He sits down on the steps, still chewing, and falls asleep, his head dropping down between his long legs, which, in this position, come almost up to his shoulders; in the distance, the faint barking of a dog, then all is quiet, apart from the muffled music from the bar. Pause.* AMÉDÉE *comes in from the left, preceded by a noise not unlike that of a tin-can attached to a dog's tail; he is labouring under the weight of the dead body, which he is pulling after him feet first; he reaches the middle of the stage. Only the legs of the dead man can be seen, the rest of the body remaining in the wings;*

he drops the feet, which make a noise as they fall; he puffs and mops his brow for a moment.]

AMÉDÉE: [*picks the feet up again and takes a step forward; noise of a tin-can; he stops; the tin-can again*] What's he up to, now! [*He pulls the feet very gently again and advances a little to the right; the tin-can is making less noise. He stops, once more out of breath.*] Now I'm half-way there . . . [*He looks round him.*] I'm in luck . . . The Square's empty. What a wonderful sky . . . If only I hadn't this wretched job to do . . .

[*He picks up the feet again and progresses a little further.*]

SOLDIER: [*looming up out of the shadows, to* AMÉDÉE] Do you speak English?

AMÉDÉE: [*rather surprised*] Oh, I'm sorry . . .

SOLDIER: Did you see Mado?

AMÉDÉE: Madeleine, my wife?

SOLDIER: No, not Madeleine, Mado . . . Do you know Mado?

AMÉDÉE: [*struggling to speak English*] Mado? . . . Mm? . . . I . . . do not . . . I . . . do . . . not . . . know . . . Mado . . .

SOLDIER: That's too bad!

AMÉDÉE: I beg your pardon? . . . What? . . .

SOLDIER: [*noticing the body, without astonishment, as naturally as possible*] Who's that? A friend? . . .

AMÉDÉE: I'm afraid I don't understand your language. Forgive me. Please don't keep me. I'm very busy.

SOLDIER: [*indicating the body*] A friend? A buddy of yours?

AMÉDÉE: Yes, yes, a friend . . . But it's none of your business. You're not a policeman . . . Ah! It's a great misfortune, the tragedy of our life . . . the skeleton in our cupboard . . . You wouldn't understand!

SOLDIER: [*who really doesn't understand*] Skeleton in your *what*? . . . I don't get it.

AMÉDÉE: I must go. I'm in a hurry. A great hurry. I don't like talking to people in the street. My wife has expressly forbidden me . . .

SOLDIER: [*still not understanding*] I see . . . I see . . .

[*He moves a few paces away.* AMÉDÉE *takes hold of the feet, pulls as hard as he can, makes little progress and stops, exhausted.*]

AMÉDÉE: I'll never do it, I'll never do it . . . And Madeleine's waiting for me . . . Oh dear . . . Perhaps I could leave him here . . . No, I can't leave him in the middle of the street . . . There'd be no room for the lorries to pass tomorrow; then there'd be an inquiry . . . they'd find out it comes from our place . . . and I'd be charged with obstructing the traffic on top of everything else . . . Oh, well! . . . Let's try again . . . [*He looks upwards for a second.*] What a beautiful sky! [*Then*] Hardly the moment . . . Try again . . . Have a look at the sky when this is over . . . when this is over . . . [*He pulls, but unsuccessfully.*] And I can't take him back to the flat either . . . it's no good, it's too much for me . . . I'm worn out . . .

SOLDIER: Wan' some help, bud?

AMÉDÉE: Please leave me alone, Monsieur, I don't want to be caught red-handed . . .

SOLDIER: No! . . .

[*By gestures he makes* AMÉDÉE *understand that he wishes to help him.*]

AMÉDÉE. Well, of course . . . If you really want to . . . thank you . . . it's most kind of you, it will be much quicker . . . I have to be back as soon as possible to finish my play . . .

SOLDIER: Play? . . .

[AMÉDÉE *shows him by sign language that he writes.*]

SOLDIER: You . . . a writer? Gee! That's swell! You're . . . writin' a play?

AMÉDÉE: Yes. A play in which I'm on the side of the living against the dead. One of Madeleine's ideas. I'm all for taking sides, Monsieur, I believe in progress. It's a problem play attacking nihilism and announcing a new form of humanism, more enlightened than the old.

SOLDIER: [*who still cannot understand*] I get it . . . I get it . . .

[*With these words the* SOLDIER *gives a tremendous pull with all his strength: a great part of the body is pulled into a heap upon the stage; the arms can be seen emerging from it and, on the left, the shoulders and the beginning of the neck. But the pull has*] *doubtless been too strong, for it has made a terrific noise and* MADELEINE'S *voice can be heard faintly from f r away.*]

MADELEINE'S VOICE: Amédée . . . What are you doing?

AMÉDÉE: [*scared*] There's that Madeleine again! Always fussing . . . [*To the* SOLDIER:] Please . . . not so hard . . . Oh dear, oh dear . . . Someone's sure to have heard . . .

[*The noise has indeed started the dogs barking and set the trains in motion: they can be heard rolling along in the distance, quietly at first, much more loudly later on. Desperately:*]

What have you done, Monsieur? You've made the dogs bark and started all the trains . . .

SOLDIER: Huh! [*Understanding*] Ah, yea, dawgs . . . I get it . . . wuff! wuff! wuff! yea . . . yea . . .

[*He seems amused by this:* AMÉDÉE *barks too, to make sure he understands he means dogs. Seeing no reason for alarm and unaware of* AMÉDÉE's *fright, the* AMERICAN *suddenly puts his finger to his brow, like someone who has a brilliant idea; then, taking hold of* AMÉDÉE *by the shoulders, he spins him round like a top.*]

AMÉDÉE: [*unable to resist*] But . . . please . . . I say . . . look here . . . [*As he realizes that the body is rolling up round his waist, he begins to spin round under his own steam so that the body shall go on rolling round him.*] Yes, thank you, that's an excellent idea . . . Americans are really quite intelligent . . . that's fine . . .

SOLDIER: [*pleased to see that* AMÉDÉE *has understood, moves aside a little to let him continue unaided*] Good, eh?

AMÉDÉE: It's much easier . . . I should have thought of it before . . . excellent idea . . . [*He stops spinning round for a moment.*] Now it's my turn to do you a favour. If ever you want to learn French, never use the sound *u* in conversation. The *u* is dangerous, it's a sharp, pointed sound. English is a soft tongue, not dangerous at all. There's no *u* in it, as there is in French.

SOLDIER: I get it . . . I get it . . .

AMÉDÉE: *U*, it's like a knife, an angle, the point of a needle, beware of it, beware . . . *u* is a whistling sound . . . If you can't avoid saying an *u*, you must round your lips into a

circle, like this, to stop it escaping. Beware of cuts or grazes,
of anything that penetrates or dislocates or pierces . . .

SOLDIER: I get it . . . I get it . . .

AMÉDÉE: . . . a cutting wit slips its barb slyly into conversation . . .
Are you a geometrician?

SOLDIER: I get it . . . I get it . . .

AMÉDÉE. In that case put yourself on the side of the spheres . . .
Choose a curve and not an angle, a circle not a triangle, an
ellipse but never a parallelepiped . . . cylinders, perhaps, but
cones only now and then . . . never pyramids as the Egyptians
did, that's what caused their downfall . . .

SOLDIER: I get it . . . I get it . . .

AMÉDÉE: And above all, evade the question . . . always move in a
circle and paraphrase and paraphrase . . . I paraphrase . . . you
paraphrase . . . we paraphrase . . . keep going round and round
or you'll have to stick to the point . . .

[*While saying these last words* AMÉDÉE *has started spinning
round again, rolling the body round and round his waist as he does
so, without a word now and growing steadily more anxious; for
this procedure is accompanied by a continuous and penetrating
whistle. But it is too late to stop, he must go on whatever happens.
In the end the whole district is astir; in the sky there is a renewed
outbreak of shooting stars, fireworks, etc.; shutters are thrown open;
windows light up and heads appear at every floor. The bar-door
opens and the owner appears on the threshold, accompanied by a
girl,* MADO, *and a Second* AMERICAN SOLDIER. *Meanwhile*
AMÉDÉE *goes on spinning round, with the body coiling round him,
and the noise of the trains and the barking of the dogs growing
louder and louder.*]

BAR-OWNER: But the trains shouldn't have started yet!

FIRST SOLDIER: [*catching sight of* MADO] Mado! Mado! Gee, what
a surprise! [*And seeing the* SECOND SOLDIER:] Hi, Bob!

[*The* FIRST SOLDIER *goes towards* MADO *and the* SECOND
SOLDIER, *who has advanced a few steps forward; he shakes them
by the hand, kisses* MADO *and is delighted to have found her again.*]

SECOND SOLDIER: Hiya, Harry!

MADO: [*to the* FIRST SOLDIER] Hallo, you. Are you the one they chucked out?

FIRST SOLDIER: Uuh?

SECOND SOLDIER: [*to the* FIRST] She wants to know if you're the one they threw out?

FIRST SOLDIER: [*jubilantly, to* MADO] Oh, yeah, that was me . . . threw me out . . . [*Pointing to the* OWNER:] That guy over there... [*He lifts* MADO *into his arms.*]

BAR-OWNER: [*from the doorway, to* AMÉDÉE] You've found a funny job for yourself! . . . Why, it's that old tenant of mine . . . it's M. Amédée . . . [*The latter is still turning, but not so easily; he is tangled up in the dead man's long legs.*] . . . Playing a game like that, at your age! . . . How's the wife? [*Someone is blowing a whistle off-stage.*] It's the cops!

AMÉDÉE: [*standing quite still, petrified*] Hell! The police!
    [TWO POLICEMEN *do, in fact, now come on at the double, blowing their whistles.*]

MADO: [*to the two* AMERICANS, *who are looking rather scared*] It's not for us . . .

FIRST POLICEMAN: [*acknowledging them as he passes*] Evening . . .
    [AMÉDÉE *turns to flee homewards, to the left, still entangled.*]

A MAN: [*at a window*] Julie . . come and look!
    [*The* POLICEMEN *run off left after* AMÉDÉE, *who has disappeared.*]

SECOND SOLDIER: [*explaining the situation to his friends*] That's a buddy of his!
    [AMÉDÉE *reappears from the left and vanishes behind the low wall at the rear, behind the bar. Shouts of laughter from the windows.*]

MADO: A pal of his? What's he doing with him, then?

BAR-OWNER: [*hands in pockets*] Now you're asking!
    [*The* TWO POLICEMEN *reappear from the left.*]

FIRST POLICEMAN: Where did he go?

SECOND POLICEMAN: Where did he go?

BAR-OWNER: [*pointing to a part of the body lying on the stage*] That's a piece of the incriminating corpse.
    [*Laughter from* MADO *and the* AMERICANS.]

A WOMAN: [*at her window*] That way, officers, he must be behind the wall! . . .

FIRST POLICEMAN: [*looking at the body*] Is that really the corpse?

SECOND POLICEMAN: Never mind that . . . Let's catch him first!
[*They run after* AMÉDÉE *and disappear behind the wall.*]

BAR-OWNER: [*to himself*] Well, M. Amédée! You're a fine one! I'd never have thought it!

A WOMAN: [*at a window*] They won't catch him!

A MAN: [*at a window*] They will!

A WOMAN: [*at a window*] No, they won't!

A MAN: [*at a window*] Yes, they will! [*To his wife, who is inside:*] Come and look, Julie! . . . There's no charge. Hurry and get up!
[*Flashes of light, stars, fireworks.*]

MADO: Ooh! Fireworks!

BAR-OWNER: [*with a shrug of his shoulders*] They're not. They're stars . . .

A WOMAN: [*at a window, to her husband, who is inside*] They won't catch him, you know . . . [*To the gentleman at the other window:*] They won't, will they, Monsieur?

MAN: [*at the window*] Want a bet on it?

FIRST SOLDIER: [*to* MADO] I'll take you along . . .

MADO: All right with me . . . To America!

FIRST POLICEMAN: [*from behind the wall, where he is invisible*] Catch him!

SECOND SOLDIER: [*to* MADO] Yeah . . . to the United States of America . . .
[*Suddenly a surprising thing happens. The body wound round* AMÉDÉE'S *waist seems to have opened out like a sail or a huge parachute; the dead man's head has become a sort of glowing banner, and* AMÉDÉE'S *head can be seen appearing above the rear wall, drawn up by the parachute; then his shoulders, his trunk and his legs follow.* AMÉDÉE *is flying up out of reach of the policeman. The banner is like a huge scarf, on which the head of the dead man is drawn, recognizable by the long beard, etc.*]

FIRST POLICEMAN: [*behind the wall*] Catch him, catch him . . . He's getting away from us . . .

AMÉDÉE: [*in flight*] Please forgive me, Ladies and Gentlemen, it's not my fault, I can't help it, it's the wind . . . Really, it's not me.

A MAN: [*at a window*] Don't often see anything like this . . .

A WOMAN: [*at a window*] He's flying away! He says he doesn't want to, but he looks quite pleased all the same.

SECOND POLICEMAN: [*jumping up from behind the wall; a hand appears, catching hold of* AMÉDÉE'S *shoe, then disappears again*] Bastard!

[*The* BAR-OWNER, MADO *and the* TWO SOLDIERS *run into the centre of the stage, where they can watch* AMÉDÉE *flying away.*]

BAR-OWNER: ⎫
MADO: ⎬ Oooh!
SOLDIERS: ⎭

[*The* AMERICANS, *naturally, pronounce this sound with a strong American accent. The* SECOND SOLDIER *quickly takes out a camera and tries to take a picture of* AMÉDÉE *in flight.*]

SECOND POLICEMAN: [*behind the wall*] All I caught was his shoe!

MADO: [*to the* SECOND AMERICAN SOLDIER] You'll give me a snap, won't you?

WOMAN: [*at the window*] I said they wouldn't catch him!

FIRST SOLDIER: [*bursting with excitement and throwing his cap into the air, as the* TWO POLICEMEN *re-appear, looking rather crest-fallen*] Hiya, boy! Hip! Hip! Hooray!

MADO AND THE PEOPLE AT THE WINDOWS: [*watching* AMÉDÉE *fly slowly away*] Oooh!

BAR-OWNER: That's what I call an escape!

FIRST SOLDIER: Attaboy! Yippee! [*He is jumping about with excitement. The* SECOND SOLDIER *has finished taking his photographs; from the windows and from all sides of the stage, applause rings out:*] Hip! Hip! Hooray!

[*One of the* POLICEMEN *is holding* AMÉDÉE'S *shoe.*]

MADO AND THE AMERICANS: Hip! Hip! Hooray!

THE PEOPLE AT THE WINDOWS: Hip! Hip! Hooray!

ALL TOGETHER: [*except the two policemen*] Hip! Hip! Hooray!

FIRST POLICEMAN: [blowing his whistle] Move along there! Move along!

   [MADELEINE appears from the left, her hair unkempt, looking quite distracted.]

MADELEINE: [running to the centre of the stage] Amédée! . . . Amédée! . . . Have you seen Amédée? What's happened to Amédée?

SECOND POLICEMAN: Is that your husband, Madame?

MADELEINE: [looking up into the sky] Heavens! It can't be! It's incredible! Is that really him?

FIRST POLICEMAN: Well, Madame, I'm afraid it is . . . Fine state of affairs!

MADELEINE: [looking into the sky] Amédée! Amédée! Amédée! Come down, Amédée, you'll catch a chill, you'll catch cold!

SECOND POLICEMAN: Amédée! Amédée! Come down, M. Amédée! Your wife's calling you!

ALL TOGETHER: Amédée! Amédée! Amédée!

   [More bursts of hilarity from the windows. AMÉDÉE re-appears, still in mid-air, on another side of the stage; everyone rushes over.]

MAN: [at the window] Hey . . . there . . . Jack-in-the-box! [To the POLICEMAN] And you there, leave him alone, can't you! Down with the police!

AMÉDÉE: I'm terribly sorry. Please forgive me, Ladies and Gentlemen . . . Please don't think . . . I should like to stay . . . stay with my feet on the ground . . . It's against my will . . . I don't want to get carried away . . . I'm all for progress, I like to be of use to my fellow men . . . I believe in social realism . . .

WOMAN: [at the window] He's a good talker.

MAN: [at the window, to his wife inside] He's making a speech . . .

AMÉDÉE: I swear to you that I'm all against dissolution . . . I stand for immanence, I'm against transcendence . . . yet I wanted, I wanted to take the weight of the world on my shoulders . . . I apologize, Ladies 'n Gentlemen, I apologize profusely.

MADELEINE: Come down, Amédée, I'll arrange things with the police . . . [*To the* POLICEMEN:] It *will* be all right, won't it?

FIRST POLICEMAN: Why yes, Madame, of course, we'll fix it all up. . . .

MADELEINE: Amédée, you can come home, the mushrooms have bloomed . . . the mushrooms have bloomed . . .

ALL TOGETHER: [*except for* AMÉDÉE] The mushrooms have bloomed . . .

FIRST SOLDIER: Hey, what are they talking about?

MAN: [*at the window, to his wife inside*] It's all about some mushrooms . . .

WOMAN: [*at the window, to her husband inside*] They're mushroom-growers . . .

AMÉDÉE: Madeleine, I promise you, you can really believe me . . . I didn't want to run away from my responsibilities . . . It's the wind, *I* didn't do anything! . . . It's not on purpose! . . . Not of my own free will!

WOMAN: [*at the window, to the* MAN *at the other window*] It's not his fault, if it's not of his own free will . . .

[AMÉDÉE *is going up, throwing down kisses as fast as he can, and says:*]

AMÉDÉE: Forgive me, Ladies and Gentlemen, I'm terribly sorry! Forgive me! [*Then*] Oh, dear! But I feel so frisky, so frisky. [*He disappears.*]

WOMAN: [*at the window*] It's a course of rejuvenation.

FIRST POLICEMAN: You might at least drop us the other shoe!

MADELEINE: [*wringing her hands*] Amédée! . . . Amédée! . . . Your career in the theatre!

MADO: Why don't you let him alone, Madame . . .

FIRST SOLDIER: [*to* MADELEINE] Off he goes . . .

MADELEINE: Amédée, Amédée, you'll make yourself ill, you haven't taken your mackintosh . . . [*Noticing the* BAR-OWNER:] Oh, good evening, Monsieur, I hadn't seen you there before! [*Then*] Amédée!

MADO: He's going to vanish into the Milky Way!

[AMÉDÉE'S *second shoe falls on the stage from above.*]

SECOND POLICEMAN: [*picking it up*] Well, that's very thoughtful!

FIRST POLICEMAN: [*to the Second*] That makes us one each!
[*They share the shoes out; then his jacket falls, and a number of cigarettes; the* POLICEMEN *rush for them, share them out between themselves and light up.*]

WOMAN: [*at the window*] He's not what you'd call stingy!

MAN: [*at the window*] Of course, it's the police that get the benefit!

WOMAN: [*at the window*] It's always the same!
[*The* POLICEMEN *offer cigarettes all round and throw them up to the people at the windows.*]

MAN: [*at the window, catching one*] Thank you, Officer.

WOMAN: [*at the window, as above*] Thank you, Officer. [*To her husband inside:*] Here you are: cigarettes!

MADELEINE: [*gazing up at the sky, which is brilliantly lit*] Come along, Amédée, won't you ever be serious? You may have gone up in the world, but you're not going up in *my* estimation!

FIRST POLICEMAN: [*looking up at the sky and wagging his finger at* AMÉDÉE, *as one would at a child*] You little rascal, you! Little rascal!

ALL TOGETHER: [*imitating the* POLICEMAN'S *gesture*] Little rascal! Little rascal!

FIRST SOLDIER: Why, Junior, you bad boy!

MADO: He's out of sight. Completely disappeared!
[*Brilliant flashes. Blazing lights from all sides.*]

BAR-OWNER: Why don't you all come and have a drink!

FIRST POLICEMAN: Why not?

MADELEINE: Oh, no! . . . I . . . I don't know if I ought to . . . I'm not thirsty!

MADO: Don't worry about it, Madame. It was the wind that did it. Men are all alike. When they don't need you any more, they leave you in the lurch! . . . Yours is nothing but a great big baby!

WOMAN: [*at the window*] He won't come back to you, Madame.

MAN: [*at the window*] He *may* come back to you . . .

WOMAN: [*at the window*] Oh, no! He won't come back. Exactly the same thing happened to me with my first husband. I never saw him again.

MADELEINE: I shall be all alone now. I don't want to marry again! And to think he never finished his play!

SECOND POLICEMAN: [*gently pushing* MADELEINE] Oh . . . People always say that . . . You never know . . . People forget . . . Why don't you come? . . . After all, the drinks are on the house . . .

MADELEINE: [*moving towards the bar with all the others*] It's such a pity! He was quite a genius, you know, really!

BAR-OWNER: All that talent wasted! It's a bad day for literature!

MADO: No one is indispensable!

[*They all go into the bar.*]

MAN: [*at the window, to his wife inside*] And *now*, *we* can go to bed . . . We've got to be up early tomorrow! . . . Come on, Julie . . .

WOMAN: [*at the window*] Let's close the shutter, Eugène, the show's over!

CURTAIN

August 1953

This is another ending to the play, which takes staging problems into account; it is easier to produce and replaces Act III, the curtain never falling at the end of Act II.

The change of scene is no longer indicated by a change of set, but by the intrusion of fresh characters on to the stage, and (at the Théâtre de Babylone) by a scenic device allowing the rear wall only of the dining-room to disappear, so that the action passes in an ill-defined space, glowing with light.

MADELEINE: Pull . . . pul-l-l . . . Why don't you pull . . . ?

AMÉDÉE: [*from far off, invisible*] I'm pul-ling . . . it's not coming very easily . . . what's the matter with it . . .

MADELEINE: [*cupping her hands*] But pul-l-l . . . you've only got to pull harder . . . Amédée . . . come on . . . pul-l-l . . . pul-l-l

. . . as har-ard . . . as you ca-an! You're not pulling as hard
as you ca-an!

AMÉDÉE: [*as before*] I'm do-o-ing . . . my-y . . . be-est . . .

MADELEINE: [*as before*] Put some stre-ength into it! . . . Why
don't you ma-ake an effort . . . Don't be so l-a-azy! . . .
[*Pause*] Th-a-t's better!

AMÉDÉE: [*as before*] Is there—still—a lot m-o-ore? M-o-ore?

MADELEINE: [*as before*] Only the h-e-ad!

[MADELEINE *is still at the window, which is almost completely
blocked; there is just enough room for her to show her head.*]

AMÉDÉE: [*as before*] I've adva-anced a little . . . I must stop to
get my brea-th! . . .

MADELEINE: [*as before*] There's no time to l-o-ose! You must be
m-a-ad . . . There's no t-i-i-me . . . you must p-u-l-l . . .
pu-l-l . . . Hurry u-u-up . . . The night is sh-o-ort . . . it'll
soon be d-a-y! . . .

AMÉDÉE: [*as before*] Just a second, only a second . . . Then I'll
have more str-ength . . . I must r-e-st . . .

MADELEINE: [*as before*] You can rest l-a-ter . . . There's no
t-i . . . ime! Pul-l-l . . . your h-e-a-rt's not in it! . . .

AMÉDÉE: [*as before*] All r-i-ght . . . I'm pu-lling . . . you must
p-u-ush to-o-o . . .

MADELEINE: [*to herself*] Can't do a thing by himself! [*She pushes
the head outwards, towards* AMÉDÉE.] Pu-l-l . . . That's right . . .
That's it . . .

AMÉDÉE: [*as before*] Is there any m-o-re? . . . P-u-ush . . . p-u-ush!

MADELEINE: [*as before*] Only the h-e-ad! . . . Where a-a-r-e
you?

AMÉDÉE: [*as before*] At the other side of the sq-u-a-re!

MADELEINE: [*cupping her hands*] Go o-on . . . go o-on! . . . once
ag-a-ain . . . ! Be c-a-areful! Don't pull the window out! [*A
violent jolt*] Not so h-a-ard! [*The walls shake.*] Not so h-a-ard,
I tell you . . . Can you hear m-e-e? You'll have the whole
h-o-use d-o-o-own . . . ! [*The whole set trembles violently*]
We'll never be able to pay the o-w-ner compens-a-ation . . .
be c-a-areful! Don't be so r-o-u-gh! L-i-sten to me, you

br-u-te! . . . Do you h-e-a-r! [*The head disappears.*] That's it!
That's it! It's out! [*To* AMÉDÉE:] It's o-o-u-t! [*A rapid glance
round the empty room*] We shall have to get some furniture
now, to furnish the flat! [*The head has disappeared completely
from view through the now empty window-frame.*] Get on the
w-a-y! The worst is o-over! And come back so-o-on! Hurry
up . . . what-ever you d-o-o . . . hu-rr-y . . . there's w-o-rk to
be d-o-one! . . . [*She gazes into the distance, shielding her eyes
with her hand.*] Amédée! Amédée! Hey! Amédée! A-a-answer
me! Let me kn-o-ow how you're getting o-o-on!

[*While* MADELEINE *is calling, watching and getting in a state,*
MADO *and the* AMERICAN SOLDIER *appear behind her. Dance
music.*]

MADO: [*wheedling*] If you teach me American, I teach you
French . . .

SOLDIER: I get it . . . I get it . . . O.K. . . . O.K.!

[MADELEINE *goes on making signs from the window.*]

MADO: [*to the* SOLDIER] You speak French?

SOLDIER: Parlez-vous anglais? . . . Je . . . parle . . . français.
Mademoiselle, Madame, Monsieur.

MADO: [*to the soldier, wantonly*] We have good time together,
you see!

MADELEINE: [*as before*] Amédée! Amédée! Amé-éd-dée!

[*While* MADO *and the* SOLDIER *are flirting, they could come up
to the window on either side of* MADELEINE, *as though she did
not exist; they talk to each other over her head and even push
her lightly aside at times in order to touch each other.*]

MADO: [*to the* SOLDIER] You speak well French?

SOLDIER: Un peu—beaucoup—passionnément.

MADO: [*simpering wantonly*] You liar . . . American liar! . . .

MADELEINE: [*shouting through cupped hands*] Amédée! . . .
A-a-answer me! . . . Where a-a-are you? [*To the* SOLDIER:]
Have you any binoculars?

SOLDIER: Uuh?

MADO: [*to the* SOLDIER] She ask you glasses . . .

SOLDIER: Oh, field-glasses. O.K! [*He hands the field-glasses to*

MADELEINE, *who looks through them into the distance; to* MADO:]
Hey, vous parlez anglais bien!

MADO: [*to the* SOLDIER] A leetle . . . you goddam son-of-a-bitch!

MADELEINE: [*with the glasses*] I can see you . . . Amédée . . .
What are you doing down there . . . You're going the wrong
way!

SOLDIER: [*to* MADO] You're a cute little baby!
[*Stretching his hand over* MADELEINE, *he caresses* MADO'S
breasts.]

MADELEINE: [*with the glasses*] Go round the corner, Amédée!
What a silly idiot! Cross the road! Don't drop him, whatever
you do!

SOLDIER: [*caressing* MADO] What's the French for these? Pample-
mousse?

MADO: [*giggling*] Grapefruit! . . . is like lemon!

MADELEINE: [*with the glasses*] Well, cro-o-oss it! There aren't any
cars about now. The road's clear! What are you w-a-i-ting
for!

MADO: [*to* MADELEINE] Oh, must you shout so loud? I can't hear
what he's saying! Can't hear ourselves speak!

MADELEINE: [*to* MADO] He's taken the wrong road! [*With the
glasses, shouting into the distance:*] . . . Amédée . . . do you hear
me? Amédée! . . .

SOLDIER: [*to* MADO, *still caressing her breasts*] Lemon or melon?

MADO: [*to the* SOLDIER] I do not mind . . . just as you like . . .
[*Simpering wantonly:*] If you satisfied . . . chéri!

SOLDIER: Lemons grow on melon-trees!
[*He kisses* MADO. *They have now taken up almost all the room at
the window;* MADELEINE *is flattened in a corner with her glasses.*]

MADO: Et vice versa!

MADELEINE: [*as before*] Amédée! Amédée! Amé-é-dée!

MADO: [*in the* SOLDIER's *arms*] Darling!

SOLDIER: Baby! [MADO *and the* SOLDIER *move slightly away from
the window, executing vague dance-steps; they stand still, then move
off again; and so they continue almost until the end of the play.*]
Lemon! Melon! Melon! Lemon!

MADELEINE: [*as before*] Look out for the curb, Amédée, and what-e-ever you do, do-o-on't trip up! Don't go near the lamp-post or you'll both be se-e-en!

SOLDIER: [*petting the girl*] And these? Pommes? Poires?

MADELEINE: [*as before*] Keep away from the *light*, Am-é-dée! . . .

MADO: Apples and pears?

MADELEINE: [*as before*] Don't make any n-o-i-se, Am-é-é-édée! Take the sh-o-rt c-u-t! The sh-o-rt c-u-t!

MADO: [*to* MADELEINE, *who does not hear her*] Oh *really*, Madame! Not so *loud*!

MADELEINE: [*as before*] Cross! . . . Turn the c-o-rner!

SOLDIER: [*to* MADO] Up those stairs!

MADO: Coucou! Coucou!

MADELEINE: [*as before*] Cross . . . turn . . . cross . . . t-u-r-n . . .

SOLDIER: [*to* MADO] Cuckoo! Cuckoo!

SOLDIER AND MADO: Cuc . . . koo . . . cou . . . cou . . . cuc . . . koo . . . cou . . . cou . . .

MADELEINE: [*as before*] Roll him round you . . . You've only got to roll him up! He'll be easier to carry! I have to teach you everything! . . . And you're not a child! [*To* MADO *and the* SOLDIER:] He has to be told everything! [*To* AMÉDÉE:] Well, roll him round you, then . . . r-o-l-l him!

MADO: [*to the* SOLDIER] Gibraltar!

SOLDIER: Casablanca!

MADELEINE: He's so awkward . . . He's turned the corner . . . what on earth can he be doing now!

SOLDIER: [*still to* MADO] Zanzibar!

MADO: Timbuctoo!

MADELEINE: What *can* he be doing! He must be wool-gathering!

SOLDIER: And these? Poppies?

MADO: Puppies?

MADELEINE: [*to the other two, who pay no attention*] He must have met someone! He'll be gossiping! And I told him not to! If you only knew how impossible he is!

SOLDIER: [*to* MADO] Puppy dogs' tails!

MADO: Ah yes! Chiens, toutous, dogs!

MADELEINE: Oh dear, oh dear, oh dear! [*She walks about the stage in great agitation.*] He must be resting at every tree!

SOLDIER: That's what little boys are made of!

MADELEINE: [*as above*] I'd better go and see! [*She puts on her hat.*] I can't leave the silly fool all alone; after all, he *is* my husband!

MADO: You're a wolf !

SOLDIER: There's a wolf around!

MADELEINE: [*hat on head*] He's a lazy hound! Oh dear, oh dear, oh dear!

SOLDIER: A wolf . . . Aouh! aouh! aouh! aouh!

MADO AND THE SOLDIER: [*holding hands*] Aouh! Aouh! Aouh! Aouh! Brrr! Aouh!

MADELEINE: He can't do a thing properly, when he's by himself ! [*While* MADO *and the* SOLDIER *go on yapping amorously at each other, a loud noise like a tin-can rattling is suddenly heard coming from* AMÉDÉE's *direction. Vehemently, much distressed:*] Ah! He's fallen down! I knew he would! I was sure of it! I should never have let him have his own way! I was quite right to try and stop him! Oh dear, oh dear! [*Into the wings:*] Get up again! ! [*Sound of a tin-can once more; furious barking breaks out in the distance.* MADO *and the* SOLDIER *go on with their little game.*] He'll wake everybody up! He'll be seen! Where is he? What'll people say! We're ruined! It's his fault! I knew this would happen! [*Noise of trains starting. Little trains can be seen moving in the backgr und.*] Now he's started up the trains! [*She returns to the window.*] Come back, Amédée! Don't leave me all alone!

[*A* MAN's *head appears at a window on one side of the stage, or emerges from the orchestra pit.*]

MAN: What's up? It's not time for the trains yet!

MADELEINE: Where are you? Come qui-i-ckly! Bring him back with you! Don't leave him in the road, he'll block the traffic! Stop star-gazing!

MAN: Making me lose my sleep! I'm a working man !

[*Whistles are being blown.*]

MADELEINE: My God, the police!

SOLDIER: Police?

MADO: Don't worry, it's not for us!

MADELEINE: There he is, running! Quick! Drop him in the road!
He won't, of course, he's stubborn as a mule!

MAN: Julie . . . get up, come and look!

   [*A* WOMAN'S *head appears next to the* MAN'S.]

WOMAN: What's up? The police?

MAN: t's M. Amédée! Funny sort of state he's in!

MADO: [*to* SOLDIER] Come and see!

MADELEINE: Make a dash for it!

WOMAN: The cops are after him! [*Confused din in the distance;
policemen's whistles.*] He's running quite fast for his age!

MADELEINE: Don't da-w-dle!

MADO: [*to the* SOLDIER] You like to see what happens in the
streets?

SOLDIER: Les rues de Paris!

WOMAN: What have they been up to now?

MAN: Can't tell, with people like that!

MADELEINE: Don't fall o-over! Run, can't you?

MAN: He's tearing across the square!

MADELEINE: Look out for the traffic lights!

SOLDIER: Oh boy, oh boy!

MAN: It's a bit of a handicap . . . a parcel like that!

MADO: They won't catch him!

WOMAN: Yes, the police'll have him!

MADO: I tell you they won't!

MADELEINE: He's round the corner! With a dog at his heels!
It'll rip his trousers! !

WOMAN: He's gone round the corner, Officer! After him!

MADO: Mind your own business!

MADELEINE: I can't see him now!

WOMAN: Behind the wall, Officer!

MAN: Don't interfere!

FIRST POLICEMAN: [*the upper part of his body only appearing, a
whistle in his hand*] Move along there !

MADELEINE: Do you hear, Amédée? Move a bit faster!

MAN: Home sweet home!

SOLDIER: Where is he?

MADO: Down there, at the corner!

MAN: They won't catch him!

SOLDIER: What a champ! Attaboy!

MADO: No!

MADELEINE: [*wringing her hands*] It's my husband! It's my husband!

WOMAN: Yes!

MAN: [*to* WOMAN] You keep out of this!

WOMAN: She says it's her husband! Why don't they keep to themselves?

POLICEMAN: Move along!

WOMAN: That way! That way!

MAN: He's got the body with him!

MADELEINE: [*running about wildly*] Drop the corpse!

POLICEMAN: Where's he gone?

   [AMÉDÉE *runs on from the back; with the dead man's hat on his head and the beard on his face.*]

WOMAN: There he goes!

MADO: There he goes!

MADELEINE: So there you are! It's about time!

   [*The* SECOND POLICEMAN *appears at the back.*]

AMÉDÉE: Don't lose your head!

FIRST POLICEMAN: [*to* SECOND POLICEMAN] Don't let him get away! Catch him!

WOMAN: Catch him!

MAN: They won't have him!

SOLDIER: Attaboy!

   [*The* SECOND POLICEMAN *tries to lay hands on* AMÉDÉE; *the* FIRST POLICEMAN *also stretches out his hand from the orchestra pit, in an attempt to catch him; but it is all in vain.* AMÉDÉE *is suddenly lifted from the ground and begins to fly.*]

FIRST POLICEMAN: [*who has caught nothing but* AMÉDÉE's *shoe*] The bastard!

MAN: ⎫
WOMAN: ⎬ Ooh!
MADO: ⎪
SOLDIER: ⎭

MADELEINE: Stop doing that, Amédée! Who told you to do that?

SECOND POLICEMAN: He's getting away!

MAN: [*to* WOMAN] I told you they wouldn't catch him!

MADO: Marvellous!

SOLDIER: [*enthusiastically*] Oh boy, oh boy!

AMÉDÉE: [*flying away*] I'm not doing it on purpose, Madeleine! I can't help myself!

FIRST POLICEMAN: All I caught is his left shoe!

MADELEINE: Oh yes, you can, you're doing it on purpose!

AMÉDÉE: [*flying away*] I promise you, Madeleine, it's not my fault, it's the wind!

MADO: You see, he says it's the wind!

MAN: It's the wind!

SOLDIER: Attaboy!

WOMAN: It's not the wind!

FIRST POLICEMAN: [*shoe in hand, to* MADELEINE *severely*] Is that your husband, Madame?

MADELEINE: Yes, officer, I'm afraid it is!

AMÉDÉE: [*slowly rising*] It's not my fault! I hope you'll all forgive me!

SECOND POLICEMAN: [*to* MADELEINE] Tell him to come down! At once!

MADELEINE: Come down at once!

MADO: [*to* MADELEINE] Why don't you leave him alone!

AMÉDÉE: [*still hanging in mid-air*] I swear it's not my fault, please forgive me, all of you, it's the wind that did it! I couldn't help myself!

MAN: Don't often see anything like this!

WOMAN: He's flying away! He says he doesn't want to, but he looks happy enough!

MADELEINE: [*to* AMÉDÉE] Will you come down at once! Do as everyone tells you!

[*The* SOLDIER *takes out a camera and photographs* AMÉDÉE *flying away.*]

SECOND POLICEMAN: A fine thing! Respectable people too!

MADO: [*to the* SOLDIER] I say, you give me one, yes?

FIRST POLICEMAN: Hi, you there! It's forbidden to take photographs!

MADELEINE: Amédée! Just you come down! You'll catch cold!

SECOND POLICEMAN: Come down, M. Amédée, your wife wants you!

MAN: Hallo, there . . . Jack-in-the-box! [*To the* POLICEMAN:] Come off it! Down with the police!

WOMAN: [*to* MAN] Aren't you ashamed of yourself?

AMÉDÉE: [*in mid-air*] I don't know what to say, please forgive me, Ladies and Gentlemen; you mustn't think . . . I should like to keep my feet on the ground . . . It's against my will . . . I don't want to get carried away . . . I should like to be of some use to my fellow men . . . I believe every man should realize his limitations . . .

MADO: Oh! He knows how to talk!

SOLDIER: Yippee! Yippee!

MAN: He's making a speech!

AMÉDÉE: [*as above*] I swear to you I'm against dissolution . . . I stand for immanence, I'm against transcendence! I'm terribly sorry . . . Please accept my apologies! . . .

MADELEINE: Listen to me, Amédée, and come down . . . I'll make it all right with the police! . . . [*To the* POLICEMEN:] Won't I?

FIRST POLICEMAN: Why yes, of course, Madame. It can all be arranged! . . .

MADELEINE: Amédée, you can come home now, the mushrooms have bloomed . . .

SOLDIER: I don't get it!

MAN: It's all about some mushrooms!

WOMAN: They're mushroom-growers!

AMÉDÉE: [*in mid-air*] Madeleine, I promise you, you can really believe me this time, I didn't want to run away from my responsibilities . . . It's the wind, I didn't do it on purpose, not of my own free will!

MADO: It's not his fault, if it's not of his own free will!

AMÉDÉE: Forgive me . . . Forgive me . . . Ladies and Gentlemen.
    [*He throws down kisses as fast as he can and flies right away.*]

FIRST POLICEMAN: [*to the vanishing* AMÉDÉE] You might at least drop the other shoe!

MADELEINE: [*wringing her hands*] Amédée, Amédée, your career in the theatre!

MADO: [*to the* SOLDIER] He must be a writer!

SOLDIER: Gee! A writer . . . that's swell! . . .

MAN: [*to* MADELEINE] Why don't you let him alone!

MADELEINE: [*to the vanished* AMÉDÉE] You've forgotten your mackintosh, you'll only make yourself ill! Amédée!
    [AMÉDÉE's *second shoe falls from on high.*]

SECOND POLICEMAN: Well, that's very thoughtful!

FIRST POLICEMAN: That makes us one each!
    [*The* POLICEMEN *take a shoe each.*]

WOMAN: And what about us?
    [*A jacket and some cigarettes fall from above.*]

MAN: Cigarettes! A jacket!
    [*They all share them out.*]

MADO: He's not what you'd call stingy! [*The sky is full of brilliant lights: comets, shooting stars, etc.*] Ooh! Fireworks!

MAN: Rockets!

WOMAN: Not real ones!

MADELEINE: [*to the sky*] Come along now, Amédée, won't you ever be serious?

SECOND POLICEMAN: [*looking up at the sky and wagging his finger at* AMÉDÉE *as one would at a child*] You little rascal, you! Little rascal!

ALL: [*imitating the* POLICEMAN's *gesture*] Little rascal! Little rascal!

SOLDIER: Why, Junior, you bad boy!
    [*Brilliant flashes. Blazing lights from all sides.*]

WOMAN: He's out of sight. He's vanished!

MADELEINE: [*to the sky*] Amédée, you haven't even finished your play!

MADO: [*to* MADELEINE] I shouldn't worry about him!

WOMAN: Men are all alike!

MADO: [*to* MADELEINE] He might come back to you!

WOMAN: Oh no! He won't come back!

[MADELEINE *turns her head from one to the other.*]

MAN: [*to* WOMAN] Why do you say that? What do you know about it?

MADO: Oh yes, he might!

WOMAN: Of course he won't! Exactly the same thing happened to me with my first husband! I never saw him again!

MADELEINE: [*to herself*] Amédée, you may have gone up in the world, but you're not going up in *my* estimation!

[*The dead man's big hat falls from above, with the beard too, if possible, and lands on* MADELEINE'*s head. She drops to the ground and sits there, the hat on her head and the beard round her neck.*]

MAN: Perhaps he was a genius!

SECOND POLICEMAN: All that talent wasted! It's a bad day for literature!

MADO: No one's indispensable!

SOLDIER: She's crying!

MADO: He's left her the flat, anyway!

SECOND POLICEMAN: Let me help you up! [*Assisting her.*] Let me buy you a drink!

MADELEINE: [*rising painfully to her feet, supported by the* POLICE-MAN, *she goes on sobbing and repeating till the end of the play*] No, no. I'm not thirsty, I'm not thirsty!

MADO: [*to the* SOLDIER] You take me to America with you?

SOLDIER: To the United States of America? . . .

MAN: [*to* WOMAN] Come on, Julie. Let's go to bed!

WOMAN: [*to* MAN] We'll close the shutters, the show's over!

FIRST POLICEMAN: [*in the orchestra pit, whistle in hand, turning towards the audience*] Move along there, please, Ladies and Gentlemen, hurry along there, move along, please . . .

CURTAIN

THE NEW TENANT

CHARACTERS:
 THE GENTLEMAN
 THE CARETAKER
 THE FIRST FURNITURE MOVER
 THE SECOND FURNITURE MOVER

THE NEW TENANT

SCENE: *A bare room, without any furniture. In the centre of the back wall, an open window. Double doors on the right and on the left. Light-coloured walls. Like the set and the furniture that will be brought on the stage later, the style of acting must be completely realistic.*

[*As the curtain rises, a considerable din is heard off stage: the sounds of voices, and hammers, snatches of song, children shouting, the noise of feet going up and coming down stairs, a barrel-organ, etc. For a moment, as the noise goes on, the stage is empty: then* THE CARETAKER *comes in from the right, crashing the door open and singing in a loud voice; she is holding a bunch of keys.*]

CARETAKER: [*as she enters singing*] La, la, la, tralalala, tralali, tralalalala-a-a! [*And rattling the keys.*] La, la, la, la! [*She interrupts her singing to go and lean out of the open window:*] Bill! Oh, Bill! Bill! Hullo there, George! Go and tell Bill 'e's got to see Mr Clarence! . . . George . . . [*Silence*] George . . . [*Silence*] Well! If 'e ain't missing too! [*She tries to lean still further out of the window, singing at the top of her voice:*] La, la, la, la, la, la, la!

[*While the row continues and* THE CARETAKER *is still craning out of the window,* THE GENTLEMAN *comes silently in from the left: he is middle-aged, with a little black moustache, dressed in dark clothes; he is wearing a bowler hat, black jacket and striped trousers, his shoes are of patent leather; he is carrying gloves, and an overcoat over one arm, and he has a little attaché-case of black leather. He closes the door quietly behind him and walks silently up to* THE CARETAKER, *who does not notice him; he stops beside her and waits for an instant without moving while* THE CARETAKER *suddenly interrupts her singing as she becomes aware of the stranger's presence; but for some moments she does not change her position and turns round only when* THE GENTLEMAN *speaks.*]

GENTLEMAN: Excuse me, are you the caretaker?

CARETAKER: [*putting her hand to her heart, she cries out*] Oh! Oh! Oh! [*And then hiccups.*] I beg pardon, Sir. I've got the hiccups. [THE GENTLEMAN *does not stir.*] 'Ave you only just come in?

GENTLEMAN: Just this moment.

CARETAKER: I was tryin' to see if Bill—or George perhaps—or someone else anyway, was in the yard . . . It's about going to see Mr Clarence. Well! . . . so you've arrived then?

GENTLEMAN: As you can see.

CARETAKER: I wasn't expectin' you, not for today I wasn't . . . I thought you was meant to come tomorrow . . . Pleased to see you, anyway. Did you 'ave a good journey? Not too tired, I 'ope? Give me quite a turn, you did! I suppose you got finished sooner than you expected! That must be it. It's just because it took me by surprise, like. [*She hiccups.*] It's the hiccups. Shock, you know. It's only what you might expect. Good thing the last lot—the people what was 'ere before you, you know—moved everything out in time. I'm not sure as 'ow I know what he used to do, mind. They said they'd send me some postcards. Worked for the government. Not a bit nervy, 'e wasn't. I suppose you wouldn't be? Would you? Don't know what department 'e worked for. I've forgot. 'E told me once. Me and them government departments! And my first 'usband was an office-boy. They was good folks. Used to

tell me everything, they did. I get used to folks' little secrets,
I do. Mum's the word for me! 'Er—the old lady, I mean—she
didn't used to work. Never lifted a finger in 'er life. I used to
look after the place for 'em, she used to 'ave someone in to
run errands for 'er and when she didn't used to come, it was
me again! [*She hiccups.*] What a fright you gave me! I wasn't
expectin' you till tomorrow. Or the day after. Used to have a
little dog, they did, they 'ated cats, but then cats isn't allowed
in this establishment. 'Course it's all the same to me, it's the
landlord what says so! Regular sort of folk they were—no
children, of course—off they'd go to the country every Sunday
to some cousins of theirs, 'olidays in Devonshire, that's where
the old gentleman come from, that's where they've gone to
live now, but they didn't used to like the cider they 'ave there
—said it used to go to their heads, liked a drop of port now and
again, just a drop, of course—*old* they were, even when they
were young—well, there it is we 'aven't all got the same ideas,
'ave we? Take me, for instance. I'm not like that. Still, they
was nice folks. And what about you? In business, are you?
Clerk? Got your own money, perhaps? Pension? Oh, but not
yet, you're too young for that, though you never know, some
of them give up early when they're tired, don't they? And
when they've *got* a little money, 'course everybody can't, good
luck to them that can, that's what I say. Got any family?

GENTLEMAN: [*laying his case and overcoat on the floor*] No, I'm
afraid not.

CARETAKER: That's right, put your case down. Nice bit of leather
—mustn't 'ave an Irishman's rest! You can put it where you
like. Well I'm blowed! 'Iccups 'ave gone! Got over me fright!
Why don't you take your 'at off and make yourself comfortable? [THE GENTLEMAN *adjusts his hat more firmly on his head.*]
Oh, I shouldn't bother to take your 'at off, Sir. Of course,
you're at 'ome now, aren't you? Last week it wasn't your
'ome yet—there's always change—it was *their* 'ome—well,
can't be helped—you 'ave to get old—it's all a question of
age—now this is *your* 'ome, I'm not the one to say it ain't—

very nice 'ere it is, a good 'ouse—must be twenty years now—
my, that's a good long stretch . . .

[*Without saying a word,* THE GENTLEMAN *takes a few paces
in the empty room, and looks around carefully, at the walls, the
doors, the ceiling: now he has his hands behind his back.*]

Ooh! They left everything proper, Sir! Clean folks they was,
really nice people. Mm? Well, of course they 'ad their faults
like you and me—bit proud they was and not what you might
call talkative, not talkative by a long chalk—never said anything much about anything to me, they didn't—only silly
things—'im—the old 'un, I mean—well, 'e was what you
might call all right—but 'er, not 'er—threw 'er cat out of the
window, she did—'it the landlord on the 'ead—what a thud!
—still, didn't 'urt my flowers. And as for 'im, 'e didn't 'alf used
to beat 'er, if you can believe it, Sir, in these days—oh, that was
their business—didn't go poking my nose in—when I come
up once, 'e was going for 'er with 'is fists, something awful
—Screaming she was, 'You brute! You bleeding bastard!'
[*She bursts out laughing: at this moment* THE GENTLEMAN *is
having a closer look at the state of the walls, still without uttering a
word; he inspects the doors and the locks, moves his hand over them,
shakes his head, etc., while the* CARETAKER *watches every movement
as she goes on talking; the din outside continues.*] Oh, I 'ad to
laugh, Sir—but there, they're away now, mustn't tell tales—
just as though they was dead, not *just* the same p'raps, specially
as it's all the same really—very nice they was, can't say I 'ad
anything to grumble about, except for New Year's Day . . .
Oh, don't you go worrying yourself about the 'ouse, Sir,
that's sound enough—this 'ouse wasn't born yesterday, don't
make 'em like that nowadays . . . You'll be all right 'ere, that
you will . . . the neighbours are good folk, it's all 'armony
'ere, always nice and quiet—I've never once 'ad to call the
police in, 'cept for the third floor front—Hinspector 'e is,
shouts out all the time, wants to arrest everybody, 'e does . . .

GENTLEMAN: [*pointing*] I beg your pardon, the window! [*In an
even, expressionless tone of voice.*]

CARETAKER: Oh, but of course, Sir—I'm only too willing to do for you. I don't ask very much, Sir. Get on fine, you an' me will, you won't 'ave any insurance stamps to worry you . . .

GENTLEMAN: [*same gesture, same calm*] The window, please!

CARETAKER: Oh yes, Sir, I *an* sorry—I was forgettin'. [*As she closes the window, there is a little less noise to be heard.*] . . . You know 'ow it is, Sir, one word leads to the next and don't time fly? [THE GENTLEMAN *continues his inspection.*] I've closed the window for you, just as you wanted—closes nice and easy. [THE GENTLEMAN *inspects the window fasteners and the window itself.*] Of course it looks out on the yard, but it's nice and bright as you can see, that's because it's on the sixth floor . . .

GENTLEMAN: There was nothing available on the ground floor.

CARETAKER: Oh! Don't think I don't know what you mean— it's no joke, the sixth floor, not when there's no lift . . .

GENTLEMAN: [*rather to himself*] That's not the point. I'm not at all tired.

CARETAKER: Oh, I see. Then why, Sir? . . . I suppose you don't like the sun? 'Course, it's true it can 'urt your eyes! When you get to a certain age, you can get on quite well without it, burns your skin right off, it does . . .

GENTLEMAN: Not at all.

CARETAKER: Well, not *right* off, of course. You 'aven't anything to sleep on tonight, 'ave you? I can lend you a bed! [*For some minutes,* THE GENTLEMAN, *still engrossed in his examination of the room, has been deciding where to put the furniture that will be arriving, pointing out to himself the various positions; he takes a tape-measure out of his pocket and starts measuring.*] I'll 'elp you to arrange the futniture, don't you worry about that, I'll give you some ideas—plenty of them about—won't be the first time, neither—since I'm going to look after you—you won't see it come today, your furnitu e, at any rate, they won't be bringing it as quick as that, just you see, I know all their little tricks, them tradespeople's all the same . . .

GENTLEMAN: Yes, indeed.

CARETAKER: *You* think they're going to bring all your things today, do you? No 'arm in *thinking*—suits me all right, I've got no bed to lend you, but mind it'd surprise *me*, 'cause I *know* 'em. My, but I've seen 'em before, this lot's not the first, they won't come, you mark my words, it's a Saturday—no, it ain't, it's a Wednesday—I've got a bed for you . . . since I'm going to do for you . . . [*She goes to open the window.*]

GENTLEMAN: If you don't mind!

CARETAKER: What's the matter? [*She turns again to open the window.*] I've got to call George to tell 'im to tell Bill to go and see Mr Clarence . . .

GENTLEMAN: Leave the window alone, please.

CARETAKER: It's all on account of Mr Clarence, what wants to know if Mr Eustace, who's a friend of Bill and George's too, since they're what you might call relations, not exactly, but in a kind of way . . .

GENTLEMAN: Please leave the window alone.

CARETAKER: All right, all right, I 'eard you, you don't want me to—wouldn't 'ave done no 'arm—you're in your rights of course, it's your window, not mine. I don't want no window—I get you, it's you gives the orders, it's just as *you* like, I won't touch it, you're the boss in your own place—don't pay much for it either—still, no business of mine—the window, that's yours, too, you can buy anything when you've got a spot of money, that's life for you—I don't say nothing, I keeps to myself, it's your affair—'ave to go down six flights of stairs now to look for Bill, poor old woman like me—Ah, well! Can't 'elp men 'aving their little ways, don't think about nothing they don't—but I'll do just what you like, you know, it's all right with me, that don't worry me, suits me fine that does, I'm going to look after you, be as though I was your servant, like, won't it, Sir?

GENTLEMAN: No, I'm afraid it won't.

CARETAKER: Beg pardon, Sir?

GENTLEMAN: I shan't be needing your services, I'm afraid.

CARETAKER: Well, I like that! After all the time you've been asking me to do for you! Bit of bad luck I didn't 'ave no

witness, took you at your word, I did, got proper took in . . .
Too kind'earted, that's me . . .

GENTLEMAN: I beg your pardon. Please don't get upset about it.

CARETAKER: Well, that's all right then.

[*A knock at the door, left.*]

GENTLEMAN: The furniture!

CARETAKER: I'll open the door. Don't you disturb yourself. I'm
the one to open the door. Must wait on you, you know. I'm
your servant. [*She goes to open the door, but* THE GENTLEMAN
steps in front of her and stops her.]

GENTLEMAN: [*still very calmly*] Please don't do anything like that!

[*He walks to the door on the left and opens it, while* THE CARE-
TAKER, *hands on hips, exclaims:*]

CARETAKER: Well, that's a bit of all right! They make up to you,
promise you the 'ole world, and then they go back on their
word!

[THE GENTLEMAN *opens the door and the* FIRST FURNITURE
MOVER *comes in.*]

FIRST FURNITURE MOVER: 'Day to you!

GENTLEMAN: Is the furniture here?

1ST FURNITURE MOVER: Can we bring it up?

GENTLEMAN: Yes, if you like.

1ST FURNITURE MOVER: Very well, Sir. [*He goes out.*]

CARETAKER: You won't never be able to arrange all that furniture
by yourself, Sir.

GENTLEMAN: That will be all right. I shall have the removal men
to help me.

CARETAKER: Well, you 'ardly want *strangers* to do it, do you?
I don't even know that one, I've never seen 'im before, it's
not safe! You ought to 'ave asked my 'ubby. Ought never to
have let 'im come in, don't do to trust no one—you never
know, you know, that's just 'ow things 'appen—foolish I
call it when there's my old man, my second you know, don't
know what 'appened to the first—he's down below, got nothing to do, 'asn't got a job—'e's 'efty enough you know, would
'elp 'im to earn a bit, why give your money away to other

people, it don't do no good, 'e could bring it up all right, 'e's tubercular you know, still, got to earn 'is bit, 'asn't 'e?—Them strikers is right, so was my first 'ubby, 'e'd 'ad enough of it, so off 'e went and then everyone's surprised!—Oh well, I'm not a bad sort really, you know, I'll look after you, wouldn't mind looking after you at all . . .

GENTLEMAN: I'm afraid I really shan't be needing your services. I'm extremely sorry. I shall be looking after myself, you see.

CARETAKER: [losing her temper and shouting] 'E says 'e's sorry, does 'e! Thinks 'e can do what he likes, does 'e!—Oooh! I don't like these sort of goings on, you can't make no fool out of me! I wish the old couple 'adn't gone, they weren't like that at all. As kind and obliging as you could wish for! They're all alike, one's as bad as another! Make you waste all your time, as though I 'adn't got nothing else to do! Tells me to come up, 'e does, and then . . .

[The noise increases off-stage, especially the sound of hammers. THE GENTLEMAN pulls a wry face; THE CARETAKER screams out into the wings.]

Don't make so much noise! I can't 'ear myself speak. [To THE GENTLEMAN:] It's all right, I'm not going to open your window, I don't want to break nobody's window-panes—I'm respectable, I am, no one never 'ad anything to say about that—So I've been wasting my time, 'ave I?—and all that washing to do, better for me if I 'adn't listened to you!

[The door on the left opens noisily and lets the 1ST FURNITURE MOVER appear, carrying two very small stools, while THE CARETAKER's tirade goes on.]

1ST FURNITURE MOVER: [to GENTLEMAN] Here's the first lot, anyway!

CARETAKER: [to the 1ST FURNITURE MOVER, who takes no notice] Don't you believe a word 'e says, my lad . . .

1ST FURNITURE MOVER: [to GENTLEMAN] Where shall I put them?

CARETAKER: [as before] . . . A pack of lies, you needn't think 'e'll pay you for it, think they can buy everything with money!

GENTLEMAN: [calmly to the 1ST FURNITURE MOVER] Would you

mind putting one of them there? And one there! [*He points either side of the door on the left.*]

CARETAKER: [*as before*] 'E'll make you sweat, 'e will.

1ST FURNITURE MOVER: [*as before*] Very good, Sir! [*He sets the stools down as directed.*]

CARETAKER: [*as before*] ... Work yourself to death, that's all life is for the likes of us ...

[*The* 1ST FURNITURE MOVER *goes out;* THE CARETAKER *turns towards* THE GENTLEMAN.]

I don't know who you *are*, but I know who *I* am. I know your sort ... Mrs Fairchild, that's me.

GENTLEMAN: [*still calm, taking money from his pocket*] Please take this for your trouble! [*Offering her money.*]

CARETAKER: Well, I never! Who do you take me for? ... I'm no pauper, wasn't my fault if I couldn't 'ave any kids, that's on account of my old man, they'd be grown up now, they would—I don't want your money! [*She takes the money and puts it in her apron-pocket.*] Very good of you, I'm sure, Sir! ... No! It's no good, you can make as much fuss as you like, you won't catch me looking after you, not the likes of you, you won't, your sort's not for me—'e don't need no one, 'e don't, wants to do it all for 'isself, 'e does—fine thing that is, too, at your time o' life ... [*She rambles on, while* THE GENTLE-MAN *walks calmly to the door on the left, exchanges the position of the two stools and moves back to judge the effect.*] ... a bad lot, that's what 'e is, a bad lot in the 'ouse, don't need nobody 'e don't, not even a blessed dog to keep 'im comp'ny—that's the sort that prowls round the streets at night—what a time to live in! Never wanted nobody like that, I didn't, fine state of affairs, we only 'ave respectable folks in our 'ouse—[*Still louder.*]—that's the sort that frightens folks on purpose when they're looking out of the window, might have broken my neck and don't need nothing 'e don't. Only wanted to pass the time o' day, don't do no one no harm, don't get much fun I don't, 'cept the pictures now and again and that's about all, don't even know what they want, they don't ... [THE GENTLEMAN, *who has finally put the stools back where they were, moves off again to admire them.*] . . . don't know much about life, that sort don't, don't do nothing but kick up a fuss . . .

GENTLEMAN: [*inspecting the stools with a satisfied look, but he is too phlegmatic to show much emotion*] Yes, they're better that way! [*The* 1ST FURNITURE MOVER *comes in through the left-hand door, noisily, with a vase in his hand.*]

CARETAKER: [*going on in the same way*] Don't 'alf 'ave a fine opinion of themselves either, they do—nothing but a lot of thieves, louts and good-for-nothings . . .

GENTLEMAN: [*to* 1ST FURNITURE MOVER] Here, you may put it here. [*Points to the left-hand corner of the stage, at the back.*]

1ST FURNITURE MOVER: There? Very good, Sir! [*Goes to the spot indicated.*]

CARETAKER: Makes all sorts of shameful suggestions to you, they does—for money . . .

GENTLEMAN: [*to* 1ST FURNITURE MOVER, *who has not put the object down right in the corner*] No! In the corner, right in the corner, there . . .

CARETAKER: That sort of lark don't cut no ice with me, not with me, it don't!

1ST FURNITURE MOVER: Here?

GENTLEMAN: Yes, there, it's fine like that . . .

CARETAKER: Oh, no! Money don't buy everything, money don't pervert everyone . . . *I* won't 'ave it any'ow!

1ST FURNITURE MOVER: [*to* THE GENTLEMAN] But where are you going to put the rest?

GENTLEMAN: [*to the* 1ST FURNITURE MOVER] Oh, please don't trouble about that, I've thought it all out, you'll see, there'll be room . . .

[*The* 1ST FURNITURE MOVER *goes off left.*]

CARETAKER: Not that it's not what I weren't expecting, your sort don't catch me napping, I know 'em, I do, all of them fine gentlemen prowling round the streets, I've got my eyes open, I 'ave, you don't catch me 'aving any, run after anything in a skirt they will, but they don't 'ave me on! I know what you're

up to, I know your little game, wanted to make a proper tart
out of me, didn't you? Me! Mother of five kids too! Fine
cheek you 'ave, come making nasty suggestions to a mother,
with five kids too—I'm not so daft as you think I am, I've got
my 'ead screwed on all right, good thing for me I 'ave.
Listen 'ere, Sir, there's a police hinspector lives right in this
very 'ouse, I'll charge you, I will, I'll 'ave you arrested, and
then there's my old man too to look after my hinterests . . .
Oh, no! Don't need nobody, 'e don't, eh? We'll see about that!

GENTLEMAN: [*who does not look at all menacing, turns towards* THE
CARETAKER; *he is extremely calm, does not raise his voice and keeps
his dignity perfectly, but he gives a surprising impression of authority*]
Please don't upset yourself! Take my advice and accept my
apologies; otherwise you will only make yourself ill!

CARETAKER: [*somewhat intimidated*] How dare you talk to me like
that! To me! Mother of five children! You won't 'ave me on
like that, you won't! Now just you listen to me! You no
sooner get 'ere and you 'ave me come upstairs, you takes me
on, and then, without not so much as a by-your-leave, you
turns me out again! When the old couple were 'ere, 'ere in this
very room where you're standing now . . .

GENTLEMAN: [*without making a gesture—his hands folded behind his
back*] May I suggest you go back to your work? The postman
may have called.

[THE CARETAKER *stops talking as though she were suddenly
really frightened;* THE GENTLEMAN, *motionless, stares at her;
then he goes back to the vase to admire it; taking advantage of
the fact that* THE GENTLEMAN'S *back is turned,* THE CARETAKER
makes a dash for the door on the right, muttering to herself.]

CARETAKER: The vase is a bit of all right! [*Then, having reached
the door, she cries in a louder voice:*] A mother of five kids! You
won't 'ave me on a bit of string! I'll go and see the hinspector,
I will! [*As she turns to go out she bumps into the* 2ND FURNITURE
MOVER, *who is just coming in.*] Watch where you're going!
[*Then she goes out, still shouting:*] You won't 'ave me on! You
won't 'ave me on!

[*While* THE GENTLEMAN *turns to the newcomer.*]

2ND FURNITURE MOVER: Good-day, Sir. I've come about your furniture, Sir.

GENTLEMAN: Ah, yes! Good morning. Thank you. Your associate is here already. [*He points to the left, over his shoulder.*]

2ND FURNITURE MOVER: Good, I'll go and help him. [*He crosses the stage towards the door on the left; as he does so he catches sight of the two little stools and the little vase in the corner, which must be about eighteen inches high.*] I see he's already started bringing them up.

GENTLEMEN: Oh, yes! He's already started bringing them up.

2ND FURNITURE MOVER: Has he been here long?

GENTLEMAN: No, only a few minutes.

2ND FURNITURE MOVER: Is there much left?

GENTLEMAN: Quite a lot, yet. [*Noise off left.*] He's coming up now.

1ST FURNITURE MOVER: [*off stage*] Are you there, Fred? Come and give me a hand, will you?

[*The* 2ND FURNITURE MOVER *goes off left, disappears for a moment and then he can just be seen coming in again backwards and straining hard; meanwhile* THE GENTLEMAN *holds out his arm to indicate different places in the room, pointing to the floor, to the walls, etc., as though it were helping him to imagine the arrangement of the furniture, saying:*]

GENTLEMAN: One . . . two . . . three . . . four . . . one . . .

[*The* 2ND FURNITURE MOVER, *coming in backwards, is almost completely visible, though it is still not possible to see what he is carrying with so much difficulty; from the wings can be heard the voice of the—*]

1ST FURNITURE MOVER: [*straining*] That's it . . . go ahead now!

GENTLEMAN: [*as before*] One . . . two . . . three . . . four . . . one . . .

[*Both* FURNITURE MOVERS *are now visible, struggling to carry between them another empty vase, identical with the first, and obviously extremely light in weight; but their united effort should appear tremendous, so much so that they are in fact stumbling under their burden.*]

1ST FURNITURE MOVER: Come on now—once more! . . .

2ND FURNITURE MOVER: Keep a good grip on it, there! . . .

GENTLEMAN: [*as before*] One . . . two . . . three . . .

1ST FURNITURE MOVER: [*to* THE GENTLEMAN] Where's this one got to go?

GENTLEMAN: [*turning towards them*] Let's see . . . yes, put it there, please! [*He points to a spot to the left of the door on the left, near the footlights.*] That's it!

[*The two* FURNITURE MOVERS *have put the vase down; they straighten up, rubbing their arms and their backs, taking off their caps to wipe their forehead; meanwhile* THE CARETAKER'S *voice can be heard from time to time raised in conversation and mixed up with other voices, but all the noise will subside gradually.*]

2ND FURNITURE MOVER: Well, I hope everything's not going to be like that!

GENTLEMAN: Are you tired, gentlemen?

1ST FURNITURE MOVER: Oh, it's nothing . . . we're used to it, you know . . . [*To his colleague:*] Mustn't waste time! Shall we go? [*They both go out through the door on the left, while—*]

GENTLEMAN: [*counting*] One . . . two . . . three . . . four . . . one . . . two . . . three . . . [*Then he moves about choosing the places to put things and someti es using the tape-measure he is holding in his hand.*]There, that will be fine . . . and we can put that there . . . and that can go here . . . That's it . . .

[*The* 1ST FURNITURE MOVER *comes in from the left carrying another vase, this time by himself but still with difficulty.* THE GENTLEMAN *points towards the other side of the stage, to the right-hand corner at the back. The* 1ST FURNITURE MOVER *goes and puts the object down, while* THE GENTLEMAN *goes on measuring:*] One . . . two . . . three . . . five . . . one . . . two . . . seven . . . Good . . . that's it . . . that'll be fine . . .

1ST FURNITURE MOVER: Is that where you want it, Sir?

[*The larger and heavier the articles that the* FURNITURE MOVERS *bring on, the easier they seem to carry them, until finally it looks like child's play.*]

GENTLEMAN: Yes, that will do nicely.

[*Then the* 1ST FURNITURE MOVER *goes off left while the* 2ND

FURNITURE MOVER *comes in through the same door, carrying another vase exactly like the rest.*]

Will you put it there, please? [*He points to the right-hand corner, near the footlights.*]

2ND FURNITURE MOVER: Ah, yes! [*He puts it down and goes off left while the* 1ST FURNITURE MOVER *comes in through the same door carrying two more tiny stools, exactly like the first ones, and still with great effort.*]

1ST FURNITURE MOVER: And where are these to go, Sir?

GENTLEMAN: [*pointing either side of the door on the right*] There and there, of course; then they'll match the two on the other side.

1ST FURNITURE MOVER: Of course, I should have thought . . . [*The* 1ST FURNITURE MOVER *sets the objects down in their place.*] Phew! Is there still any room left? [*He stops for a moment, with nothing in his hands, in the middle of the room, then he goes off left.*]

GENTLEMAN: There'll be enough. There's sure to be enough. I have it all worked out. [*To the* 2ND FURNITURE MOVER, *who enters from the left, with a suitcase:*] Put it there please . . . [*He points to the right of the window at the back; as the* 2ND FURNITURE MOVER *moves towards the spot,* THE GENTLEMAN *stops him.*] I'm sorry. Not there. There . . . [THE GENTLEMAN *points to the left of the window; the* 2ND FURNITURE MOVER *sets the object down, saying:*]

2ND FURNITURE MOVER: Right, Sir. It would help if you could be a little more definite, Sir.

GENTLEMAN: Why, yes, of course.

2ND FURNITURE MOVER: And then we won't tire ourselves out unnecessarily.

GENTLEMAN: Of course, I understand.

1ST FURNITURE MOVER: [*coming in from the left with a pedestal table while the* 2ND FURNITURE MOVER *goes out left*] And this? Where shall I put this?

GENTLEMAN: Ah yes . . . let me see . . . it's not easy to find the right little place for that . . .

1ST FURNITURE MOVER: Here, perhaps, Sir! [*He carries the table to the left of the window.*]

GENTLEMAN: The ideal place! [*These tables are all in different shapes and colours.*] Ideal!

2ND FURNITURE MOVER: [*coming in left with another pedestal table*] And this?

GENTLEMAN: [*indicating a place to the left of the first table*] Here, if you don't mind.

2ND FURNITURE MOVER: [*puts it down*] But there won't be any room for your plates!

GENTLEMAN: Everything's been accounted for.

2ND FURNITURE MOVER: [*looking round the stage*] I don't quite see ...

GENTLEMAN: Yes, I assure you.

2ND FURNITURE MOVER: Well, if you say so. [*He goes off left, while the 1ST FURNITURE MOVER arrives, with another table.*]

GENTLEMAN: [*to 1ST FURNITURE MOVER*] Beside the last one. [*Then while the 1ST FURNITURE MOVER places the table in position and goes out, and the 2ND FURNITURE MOVER comes in, still from the left, with another table, THE GENTLEMAN traces a circle on the floor in chalk; then, more carefully, a larger circle in the middle of the stage; THE GENTLEMAN stops and straightens up to show the 2ND FURNITURE MOVER where to put his latest pedestal table:*] There, along by the wall, next to the other! [*While the 2ND FURNITURE MOVER puts it down, THE GENTLEMAN, who has finished tracing his circle, straightens up again and says:*] That will be fine! [*While the 2ND FURNITURE MOVER goes off, still on the left, the 1ST FURNITURE MOVER arrives with another pedestal table:*] Next to the last one!

[*He points out the place, the 1ST FURNITURE MOVER puts it down and goes off left. THE GENTLEMAN, alone for a moment, counts the pedestal tables.*]

Yes ... that's it ... now we shall have to ... [*The 2ND FURNITURE MOVER comes in from the right with another pedestal table.*] All round the room ... [*Then, from the left, the 1ST FURNITURE REMOVER.*] All around ...

[*Both FURNITURE MOVERS go off, the 1ST on the left, to come on again from the right, the* 2ND *on the right, to come in again from the left, and they bring on more tables and other objects such as chairs, screens, table-lamps, piles of books, etc., which they set down, one after the other, all round the stage and along the walls, meeting and passing each other as they do so. The movement is carried out in such a way that there is always one* FURNITURE MOVER *on the stage throughout the scene that follows.*]

All around the room, all around . . . all around . . . [*Then, when the walls are all lined with the first row of furniture,* THE GENTLEMAN *says to the* 1ST FURNITURE MOVER, *who comes in, empty-handed, from the left:*] Now you can bring a step-ladder! [*The* 1ST FURNITURE MOVER *goes out the way he came in, the* 2ND FURNITURE MOVER *comes on from the right.*] A step-ladder! [*The* 2ND FURNITURE MOVER *goes out the way he came in.* THE GENTLEMAN *is looking round the walls and rubbing his hands together:*] There now! Now it's beginning to take shape. It'll be a very comfortable sort of place. It won't be at all bad.

[*The two* FURNITURE MOVERS *come in from the left and right, each from the side opposite to the one they went out;* THE GENTLEMAN *indicates to the one coming from the left the wall on the right, and vice-versa; he says nothing.*]

1ST FURNITURE MOVER: Right ho!

2ND FURNITURE MOVER: Right ho!

[*They cross and place their ladders against the walls indicated.*]

GENTLEMAN: Leave the ladders there. You can bring in the pictures now! [*They come down their ladders and go off right and left. As he moves towards the exit, the* 2ND FURNITURE MOVER *steps on one of the chalk circles, the one in the middle of the stage.*] Be careful there! Don't spoil my circle.

2ND FURNITURE MOVER: Oh, yes! We'll try not to.

GENTLEMAN: Be careful! [*The* 2ND FURNITURE MOVER *goes out while the* 1ST FURNITURE MOVER *enters from the opposite side with a large painting representing the head of a hideous old man.*] Be careful, be careful of my circles. [*This said in a calm and neutral tone.*]

1ST FURNITURE MOVER: I'll try. It's not easy when you're loaded . . .

GENTLEMAN: Now hang the picture up . . .

1ST FURNITURE MOVER: Yes, Sir. [*He climbs up the ladder and carefully hangs the picture. The* 2ND FURNITURE MOVER *enters from the side opposite the one from which the* 1ST FURNITURE MOVER *has just come in, also carrying a large painting representing another hideous old man.*]

GENTLEMAN: My ancestors. [*To the* 2ND FURNITURE MOVER:] Now go up the ladder and hang the picture.

2ND FURNITURE MOVER: [*going up the ladder against the opposite wall, holding the picture*] It's not easy, with all your circles. Especially when we come to the heavy objects. We can't watch out for everything. [*He busies himself hanging the picture.*]

GENTLEMAN: Oh yes, you can, if you really want to. [THE GENTLEMAN *picks up from amongst the various objects brought on the stage a book or a box or some other still smaller object and takes it to the centre of the stage where he sets it down after having inspected it by raising it above his head; meanwhile, the workmen are busy fixing the paintings carefully on the two walls;* THE GENTLEMAN *could also adjust the position of some of the furniture slightly or retrace his chalk circles again; all this without a word spoken. A slight sound of hammers and the other exterior noises can still be heard, but already transformed into music.* THE GENTLE-MAN *contemplates the painting and the room in general with an air of satisfaction. The two workmen have finished, and so has* THE GENTLEMAN: *the work should have lasted some time, acted without words. The* FURNITURE MOVERS *come down from their ladders; they go and put the ladders where there is still a little space, as for example near the two doors; then they join* THE GENTLEMAN, *who studies first one of the pictures, then the other.*]

1ST FURNITURE MOVER: [*pointing to the two pictures, speaking to* THE GENTLEMAN] All right?

GENTLEMAN: [*to* FURNITURE MOVER] All right?

2ND FURNITURE MOVER: Looks all right to me.

GENTLEMAN: [*inspecting the pictures*] They're firmly fixed. [*Pause*] Bring in the heavy objects.

2ND FURNITURE MOVER: It's thirsty work! [*Mops his brow.*]

GENTLEMAN: We must have the sideboard then. [*Both* FURNITURE MOVERS *go towards the door on the right;* THE GENTLEMAN *turns towards the window.*] One . . . yes . . . one here . . .

[*Before the two* FURNITURE MOVERS *can reach the door on the right, the two folding doors open of themselves and a sideboard slides onto the stage, propelled by an invisible force; the folding doors close again and the* FURNITURE MOVERS *seize the sideboard and glance towards* THE GENTLEMAN, *who with a gesture shows them where to put it.*]

BOTH FURNITURE MOVERS: [*who are now near the centre of the stage*] Where?

GENTLEMAN: [*his back to the audience, his hands extended towards the window*] But there, of course! . . .

1ST FURNITURE MOVER: You'll shut out all the light.

GENTLEMAN: There's electric light, isn't there?

[*The* 1ST FURNITURE MOVER *pushes the sideboard against the window; it fails to block it up completely; it is not high enough. The* 2ND FURNITURE MOVER *goes to one of the doors and switches on the ceiling light; he takes hold of a picture representing a winter landscape, which has glided on to the stage by itself through the folding doors, and places it on top of the sideboard: this time the window is completely masked. The* 1ST FURNITURE MOVER *opens the sideboard, takes a bottle out, takes a swig from it, passes it to the* 2ND FURNITURE MOVER, *who does the same, and then offers it to* THE GENTLEMAN.]

No, thank you. I never touch it.

[*Then both the* FURNITURE MOVERS *drink in turn out of the bottle, handing it backwards and forwards, and looking at the blocked-up window.*]

Much better, like that.

[*The two* FURNITURE MOVERS, *too, still drinking from time to time, turn to face the window concealed by the sideboard and the canvas representing winter, so that, in this way, all three have their backs to the audience.*]

1ST FURNITURE MOVER: [*with approval*] Ah ha!

2ND FURNITURE MOVER: [*with approval*] Ah ha!

GENTLEMAN: It's not quite right [*Indicating the picture.*] I don't like it . . . Turn it round!

> [*The two* FURNITURE MOVERS *turn the picture round while* THE GENTLEMAN *watches them; only the back of the picture is to be seen, with its dark frame and hanging cord; then the two* FURNITURE MOVERS *step away a little and again pick up the bottle and go on drinking; then they go and stand on either side of* THE GENTLEMAN, *still with their backs to the audience, and again gaze at the sideboard with the picture on top of it in silence for several moments.*]

I like it better like that.

1ST FURNITURE MOVER: It's much nicer.

GENTLEMAN: Much nicer. More restrained.

2ND FURNITURE MOVER: Much nicer. More restrained.

GENTLEMEN: Ah, yes, it's very much nicer, more restrained.

1ST FURNITURE MOVER: Ah yes . . .

2ND FURNITURE MOVER: Ah yes . . .

GENTLEMAN: You can't see anything now.

1ST FURNITURE MOVER: Well, that's something.

> [*Silence*]

2ND FURNITURE MOVER: [*after a moment, turning the bottle neck downwards*] There isn't any more.

1ST FURNITURE MOVER: The last drop.

2ND FURNITURE MOVER: [*still holding the bottle in the same way, to* THE GENTLEMAN] There isn't any more.

GENTLEMAN: I don't think so either. [*The* 1ST FURNITURE MOVER *takes the bottle from the* 2ND FURNITURE MOVER *and puts it in the sideboard, which he closes.*] Won't have any more trouble from the neighbours now.

1ST FURNITURE MOVER: Better for everybody.

2ND FURNITURE MOVER: Everybody will be happy.

GENTLEMAN: Everyone will be happy. [*A moment of silence.*] To work. Let's go on. My armchair.

1ST FURNITURE MOVER: Where can we put it?

2ND FURNITURE MOVER: Where can we put it?

GENTLEMAN: In the circle. [*He points to the circle in the middle.*] You won't be able to spoil my circle any more.

1ST FURNITURE MOVER: [*to* THE GENTLEMAN] You'll be able to see it better.

GENTLEMAN: [*to the* 1ST FURNITURE MOVER] Will you go and fetch it?

[*The* 1ST FURNITURE MOVER *goes to the door on the right. To the* 2ND FURNITURE MOVER:] Now for the heavy furniture in pink wood.

[*The* 1ST FURNITURE MOVER *arrives at the door on the right; the armchair glides on, pushed from behind; he takes hold of it. The* 2ND FURNITURE MOVER *goes to the door on the left; half a wardrobe appears; he seizes hold of it and pulls it towards the centre of the stage; all the movements have slowed down; from now on all the furniture comes on through the two doors alternately, propelled from behind; each item only half appears; the* FURNITURE MOVERS *pull it towards them, and when it has been pulled right into the room, something else slides on, half visible, and so on. The* 1ST FURNITURE MOVER, *then, has hold of the armchair, while the other man is pulling through the other doorway a huge wardrobe lying on its side; the* 1ST FURNITURE MOVER *sets the armchair down within the circle.*]

GENTLEMAN: [*looking at the pink wardrobe*] It's a beautiful pink, isn't it?

1ST FURNITURE MOVER: [*after placing the armchair within the circle*] Good armchair.

GENTLEMAN: [*feeling the upholstery*] Yes, it's very soft. Well-upholstered. [*To the* 1ST FURNITURE MOVER:] Please don't stop bringing the things in. [*The* 1ST FURNITURE MOVER *goes to the door on the right, where he finds a second pink wardrobe on its side; the* 2ND FURNITURE MOVER, *still dragging his wardrobe on, glances at* THE GENTLEMAN, *as though asking silently where to put it.*]

There!

[*The wardrobes in question—there could be four in all—will be disposed, always according to* THE GENTLEMAN'S *directions,*

*along the three walls, parallel to the other rows of furniture;
first one, then the other of the two* FURNITURE MOVERS *will dart
a questioning look at* THE GENTLEMAN *each time they have
succeeded in dragging the furniture clear of the folding doors and*
THE GENTLEMAN *will point and say to them:*]

There! There! There! There!

[*At each 'There!', the* FURNITURE MOVERS *nod their heads
affirmatively and bring the furniture in; after the four wardrobes
come smaller items—some more tables, settees too, wickerwork
baskets,* strange furniture never seen before, *etc. It is all placed
in front of the rest along the three walls, so that* THE GENTLEMAN
*is confined in an ever-diminishing space in the centre of the stage;
the action is like a ponderous kind of ballet and all the movements
are made very slowly.*

While the FURNITURE MOVERS *are still bringing on the furniture
and questioning him silently, while the furniture is still sliding on
to the stage, pushed on from behind,* THE GENTLEMAN *is in the
centre, with one hand on the back of the armchair and the other
pointing:*]

There . . . There . . . There . . . There . . . There . . . There
. . . There . . . There . . . There . . . There . . . There . . .
There . . . There . . . There . . . There . . . There . . . [*It should
be arranged so that this action lasts a long time; in a slow and broken
rhythm. Then, at a certain moment, the* 1ST FURNITURE MOVER
*brings on a radio set from the right; when his questioning glance
alights on* THE GENTLEMAN, *the latter says, in a voice scarcely
louder than before:*] Oh no! Oh dear me no!

1ST FURNITURE MOVER: It doesn't work.

GENTLEMAN: Well, in that case . . . yes. Here. [*He indicates a
spot near the armchair; the* 1ST FURNITURE MOVER *deposits the
article and moves off towards the right for more, while the* 2ND
FURNITURE MOVER *comes up from the left, with the same look of
interrogation, carrying a chamber-pot; to the* 2ND FURNITURE
MOVER:] Why yes, of course . . . here.

[*He points to the other side of the armchair; the* 2ND FURNITURE
MOVER *lays the chamber-pot down and then they both move off*

*their own side and come back again with other furniture so that
the space surrounding* THE GENTLEMAN *gets smaller and smaller;
now the action continues without words, in complete silence; little
by little the sounds from outside,* THE CARETAKER'S *voice, etc.,
have died away; the* FURNITURE MOVERS *pad about noiselessly;
the furniture appears on the stage quite silently; each time the*
FURNITURE MOVERS *introduce a new item they still look question-
ingly at* THE GENTLEMAN *and the latter still indicates by gesture,
without uttering a word, where to put the various articles, which
are slowly but surely closing in on him. This dumb show, with its
broken mechanical movements, should also last a long time, even
longer, perhaps, than the previous scene of* THE GENTLEMAN'S
'There . . . There . . . There . . . There': finally the 2ND
FURNITURE MOVER *brings on an enormous wall-clock from the
left, while the other* FURNITURE MOVER *continues as before; when*
THE GENTLEMAN *sees the clock, he shows surprise and uncertainty,
then finally makes a sign of refusal; while the* 2ND FURNITURE
MOVER *takes the clock away to bring up another piece of
furniture the* IST FURNITURE REMOVER *arrives with a second
clock that resembles the first in every respect;* THE GENTLEMAN
dismisses him with a gesture, then changes his mind.]

GENTLEMAN: But wait . . . after all, why not? [*The clock is brought
up to the armchair, and* THE GENTLEMAN *points to a place near
it; next the* 2ND FURNITURE MOVER *comes back with a large
and very high screen; as he reaches the armchair the* IST FURNI-
TURE MOVER *comes up from his side also carrying a screen of
the same height.*]

2ND FURNITURE MOVER: There'll be no room left!

GENTLEMAN: Oh, yes, there will. [*He sits down in his armchair
within the circle.*] Like this there will.

[*The* FURNITURE MOVERS *bring up a second and then a third
screen and enclose* THE GENTLEMAN *on three sides, within the
circle. Only the side facing the audience remains open.* THE
GENTLEMAN *is sitting in the armchair, with his hat on his head,
his face turned towards the public; on each side, the two* FURNITURE
MOVERS, *their bodies hidden behind the screens, poke their heads*

round to have a look at THE GENTLEMAN.]

1ST FURNITURE MOVER: All right? You comfortable now?

[THE GENTLEMAN *nods his head.*]

It's good to feel at home.

2ND FURNITURE MOVER: You must have got tired. I should have a little rest.

GENTLEMAN: Don't stop, will you? . . . Is there still much left?

[*Dumb show.* THE GENTLEMAN *is seated, motionless, hat on head, facing the audience; the two* FURNITURE MOVERS *make their way, each to one of the two entrances; the folding doors are wide open; the two openings are completely blocked and one can only see great wooden boards, green on the left, purple on the right, as high as the doors themselves, apparently the backs of tall, wide wardrobes; synchronizing their movements, each man looks at the door in front of him and scratches his head underneath his cap in a puzzled way; they shrug their shoulders and put their hands on their hips simultaneously; then, still moving together, they step back amongst the furniture, each man on his own side of the stage and gape at each other. Then:*]

1ST FURNITURE MOVER: What shall we do?

2ND FURNITURE MOVER: What shall we do?

GENTLEMAN: [*without moving*] Is there still much left? Isn't it finished yet?

[*The* 1ST FURNITURE MOVER, *without answering* THE GENTLE-MAN, *makes a meaningful gesture directed at the* 2ND FURNITURE MOVER, *a gesture expressing bewilderment, which the* 2ND FURNITURE MOVER *repeats. Without moving, still very calm:*]

Have you brought up *all* the furniture?

[*Dumb show for a moment. Both* FURNITURE MOVERS, *still standing where they were, turn towards their respective doors, and then towards* THE GENTLEMAN, *who can no longer see them.*]

1ST FURNITURE MOVER: It's really rather awkward, Sir.

GENTLEMAN: What is?

2ND FURNITURE MOVER: The rest of the furniture's very big and the doors aren't.

1ST FURNITURE MOVER: Can't get it in.

GENTLEMAN: What is it that's left?

1ST FURNITURE MOVER: Wardrobes.

GENTLEMAN: The green and the purple ones?

2ND FURNITURE MOVER: Yes.

1ST FURNITURE MOVER: And that's not all. There's more to come.

2ND FURNITURE MOVER: The staircase is jammed from top to bottom. Nobody can get up or down.

GENTLEMAN: The yard is cram-full too. So is the street.

1ST FURNITURE MOVER: The traffic's come to a standstill in the town. Full of furniture.

2ND FURNITURE MOVER: [to THE GENTLEMAN] At least you've nothing to complain about, Sir. You've got somewhere to sit.

1ST FURNITURE MOVER: Perhaps the tube's still running.

2ND FURNITURE MOVER: No, it isn't.

GENTLEMAN: [still as before] No. All the underground lines are blocked.

2ND FURNITURE MOVER: [to THE GENTLEMAN] Some furniture! It's cluttering up the whole country.

GENTLEMAN: The Thames has stopped flowing, too. Dammed up. No more water.

1ST FURNITURE MOVER: What can we do then, if we can't get any more in?

GENTLEMAN: It can't be left outside, because of the weather.

[The FURNITURE MOVERS are still speaking from their respective positions.]

1ST FURNITURE MOVER: Might be able to get it in through the attic. But then . . . we'd have to break the ceiling in.

2ND FURNITURE MOVER: Not necessary. Modern house. Sliding ceiling. [To THE GENTLEMAN:] Did you know?

GENTLEMAN: No.

2ND FURNITURE MOVER: Well, there you are. It's easy. Just have to clap your hands. [He makes the gesture.] The ceiling opens.

GENTLEMAN: [from his armchair] No . . . I'm afraid of the rain on the furniture. It's new and easily spoilt.

2ND FURNITURE MOVER: No fear of that, Sir. I know how it works. The ceiling opens and closes, opens and closes, just as you want.

1ST FURNITURE MOVER: Come on then, perhaps we can . . .

GENTLEMAN: [*from his armchair*] Providing you close it again at once. No carelessness, mind.

1ST FURNITURE MOVER: We won't forget. *I'm* on the job. [*To the* 2ND FURNITURE MOVER:] Ready?

2ND FURNITURE MOVER: Yes.

1ST FURNITURE MOVER: [*to* THE GENTLEMAN] All right?

GENTLEMEN: Right.

1ST FURNITURE MOVER: [*to the* 2ND FURNITURE MOVER] Go ahead.

[*The* 2ND FURNITURE MOVER *claps his hands. From the ceiling huge planks descend at the front of the stage, completely hiding from view* THE GENTLEMAN *in his high-walled enclosure; a few could also come down on to the stage amongst the furniture; the new tenant is thus completely walled-in; clambering over the furniture the* 1ST FURNITURE MOVER, *after knocking three times without response on one of the screens at the side, makes his way, with a ladder, to the place where the planks have completed the enclosure; he holds in one hand a bunch of flowers that he tries to hide from the audience; silently he leans his ladder up against the end plank on the right; when he has reached the top, he looks down into the enclosure and calls out to* THE GENTLEMAN:]

That's it, Sir. Everything in. Are you nice and comfortable? Has the move gone off to your satisfaction?

GENTLEMAN'S VOICE: [*just as it has always been; slightly muffled, that's all*] Ceiling. Close ceiling, please.

1ST FURNITURE MOVER: [*from the top of the ladder to his mate*] He wants you to close the ceiling. You forgot.

2ND FURNITURE MOVER: [*in the same spot*] Oh, yes. [*He claps for the ceiling to close again.*] There you are.

GENTLEMAN'S VOICE: Thank you.

1ST FURNITURE MOVER: [*on the ladder*] Ah well, you've got a good sheltered spot there, you won't be cold . . . Are you all right?

GENTLEMAN'S VOICE: [*after a silence*] All right.

1T FURNITURE MOVER: Hand me your hat, Sir, it might worry syou.

[*After a short pause,* THE GENTLEMAN's *hat can be seen appearing from within the enclosure.*]

1ST FURNITURE MOVER: [*taking the hat and throwing the flowers down inside*] That's right. You'll be more comfortable like that. Here are some flowers for you. [*To the* 2ND FURNITURE MOVER:] Is that all?

2ND FURNITURE MOVER: That's all.

1ST FURNITURE MOVER: Good. [*To* THE GENTLEMAN:] We've brought everything, Sir, you're really at home now. [*He comes down off the ladder.*] We'll be off. [*He leans the ladder against the wall, or perhaps he can prop it up, gently, without making a noise, somewhere amongst the other objects that hem* THE GENTLEMAN *in. To the* 2ND FURNITURE MOVER:] Come on.

[*The two* FURNITURE MOVERS, *each still keeping to his own side, make their way, blindly and tentatively, to the back of the stage, towards invisible and problematical exits, Heaven knows where; for the window is stopped up and through the open folding doors you can still see the violently coloured wood that blocks the way.*]

1ST FURNITURE MOVER: [*at a certain moment, he stops,* THE GENTLEMAN's *hat in his hand, turns round and directs his words from one end of the stage towards the concealed* GENTLEMAN] Is there anything you want?

[*Silence*]

2ND FURNITURE MOVER: Is there anything you want?

GENTLEMAN's VOICE: [*after a silence; not a movement on the stage*] Put out the light. [*Utter darkness.*] Thank you.

CURTAIN

VICTIMS OF DUTY

A PSEUDO-DRAMA

CHARACTERS:
 CHOUBERT
 MADELEINE
 THE DETECTIVE
 NICOLAS D'EU
 THE LADY
 MALLOT *with a t.*

VICTIMS OF DUTY

A PSEUDO-DRAMA

SET: A petit bourgeois *interior*. CHOUBERT *is sitting in an armchair near the table reading a newspaper.* MADELEINE, *his wife, is sitting at the table darning socks.*

[*Silence*]

MADELEINE: [*pausing in her work*] Any news in the paper?

CHOUBERT: Nothing ever happens. A few comets and a cosmic disturbance somewhere in the universe. Nothing to speak of. The neighbours have been fined for letting their dogs make a mess on the pavement . . .

MADELEINE: Serve them right. It's horrible when you step on it.

CHOUBERT: And think of the people on the ground floor, opening their windows in the morning to see *that*! Enough to put them in a bad mood for the rest of the day.

MADELEINE: They're *too* sensitive.

CHOUBERT: It's the times we live in; all nerves. Nowadays men

have lost the peace of mind they had in the past. [*Silence*]
Oh, and here's an official announcement.

MADELEINE: What's it say?

CHOUBERT: It's quite interesting. The Government's urging all
the citizens of the big towns to cultivate detachment. According
to this, it's our last hope of finding an answer to the economic
crisis, the confusion of the spirit and the problems of existence.

MADELEINE: We've tried everything else, and it hasn't done any
good, but I don't suppose it's anyone's fault.

CHOUBERT: For the time being the Government's merely
recommending this ultimate solution in a friendly manner.
They can't fool us; we know how a recommendation has a
way of turning into an order.

MADELEINE: You're always so anxious to generalize!

CHOUBERT: We know how suggestions suddenly come to look
like rules, like strict laws.

MADELEINE: Well, my dear, you know, the law *is* necessary,
and what's necessary and indispensable is *good*, and everything's that good is *nice*. And it really is very nice indeed to
be a good, law-abiding citizen and do one's duty and have a
clear conscience! . . .

CHOUBERT: Yes, Madeleine. When one really thinks about it,
you're right. There is something to be said for the law.

MADELEINE: Of course there is.

CHOUBERT: Yes, yes. Renunciation has one important advantage:
it's political and mystical at the same time. It bears fruit on
two levels.

MADELEINE: So you can kill two birds with one stone.

CHOUBERT: That's what's so interesting about it.

MADELEINE: You see!

CHOUBERT: Besides, if I remember rightly from my history
lessons, this system of government, the 'detachment system',
has already been tried before, three centuries ago, and five
centuries ago, nineteen centuries ago, too, and again last
year . . .

MADELEINE: Nothing new under the sun!

CHOUBERT: . . . successfully too, on whole populations, in capital cities and in the countryside, [*He gets up.*] on nations, on nations like ours!

MADELEINE: Sit down. [CHOUBERT *sits down again.*]

CHOUBERT: [*sitting*] Only, it's true, it *does* demand the sacrifice of some of our creature comforts. It's still rather a nuisance.

MADELEINE: Oh, not necessarily! . . . Sacrifice isn't always so difficult. There's sacrifice *and* sacrifice. Even if it *is* a bit of a nuisance right at the start, getting rid of some of our habits, once we're rid of them, we're rid of them, and you never really give them another thought!

[*Silence*]

CHOUBERT: You're often going to the cinema; you must be very fond of the theatre.

MADELEINE: Of course I am, just like everyone else.

CHOUBERT: *More* than everyone else.

MADELEINE: Yes, more.

CHOUBERT: What do you think of the modern theatre? What are your ideas on the drama?

MADELEINE: You and your theatre! It's an obsession, you'll soon be a pathological case.

CHOUBERT: Do you really think something new can be done in the theatre?

MADELEINE: I've just told you there's nothing new under the sun. Even when there isn't any.

[*Silence*]

CHOUBERT: You're right. Yes, you're right. All the plays that have ever been written, from Ancient Greece to the present day, have never really been anything but thrillers. Drama's always been realistic and there's always been a detective about. Every play's an investigation brought to a successful conclusion. There's a riddle, and it's solved in the final scene. Sometimes earlier. You seek, and then you find. Might as well give the game away at the start.

MADELEINE: You ought to quote examples, you know.

CHOUBERT: I was thinking of the Miracle Play about the woman

Our Lady saved from being burned alive. If you forget that bit of divine intervention, which really has nothing to do with it, what's left is a newspaper story about a woman who has her son-in-law murdered by a couple of stray killers for reasons that are unmentioned . . .

MADELEINE: And unmentionable . . .

CHOUBERT: The police arrive, there's an investigation and the criminal is unmasked. It's a thriller. A naturalistic drama, fit for the theatre of Antoine.

MADELEINE: That's it.

CHOUBERT: Come to think of it, there's never been much evolution in the theatre.

MADELEINE: Pity.

CHOUBERT: You see, the theatre's a riddle, and the riddle's a thriller. It's always been that way.

MADELEINE: What about the classics?

CHOUBERT: Refined detective drama. Just like naturalism.

MADELEINE: You've got some original ideas. Perhaps there's something in them. Still, you ought to get an expert opinion on the subject.

CHOUBERT: Who from?

MADELEINE: Oh, there's bound to be someone, among the cinema enthusiasts, or the professors at the *Collège de France*, the influential members of the Agricultural School, the Norwegians or some of those veterinary surgeons . . . A vet, now there's someone who should have lots of ideas.

CHOUBERT: Everyone's got ideas. No shortage there. But it's facts that count.

MADELEINE: Facts, nothing but facts. Still, we could ask them what they think.

CHOUBERT: We'll *have* to ask them.

MADELEINE: We must give them the time to think about it. You've *got* the time . . .

CHOUBERT: It's a fascinating subject.

[*Silence.* MADELEINE *darns socks.* CHOUBERT *reads his paper. Someone is heard knocking at a door, but not one of the doors of the room they are in.* CHOUBERT, *however, raises his head.*]

MADELEINE: It's the other side, for the concierge. She's never there.

[*The knocking is heard again. The door of the concierge's place is probably on the same landing. Then:*]

DETECTIVE'S VOICE: Concierge! Concierge!

[*Silence. Again there is knocking, and again.*]

Concierge! Concierge!

MADELEINE: She's *never* there. We're so badly looked after!

CHOUBERT: A concierge ought to be chained to her room. I expect it's for one of the tenants. Shall I go and see?

[*He gets up and sits down again.*]

MADELEINE: [*quite quietly*] It's no business of ours. Neither of us is a concierge, you know. Everyone in society has his own special duty to perform!

[*Short silence.* CHOUBERT *reads his paper.* MADELEINE *darns her socks. Gentle tapping on the right-hand door.*]

CHOUBERT: This time, it's for us.

MADELEINE: You can go and see, dear.

CHOUBERT: I'll open the door.

[CHOUBERT *gets up, walks to the right-hand door and opens it. The* DETECTIVE *is seen in the doorway. He is very young, with a brief-case under one arm. He is wearing a beige overcoat and is hatless, a fair man, soft-spoken and excessively shy.*]

DETECTIVE: [*in the doorway*] Good evening, Monsieur. [*Then to* MADELEINE, *who has also risen and moved to the door:*] Good evening, Madame.

CHOUBERT: Good evening. [*To* MADELEINE:] It's the Detective.

DETECTIVE: [*taking one short timid step forward*] Forgive me, Madame, Monsieur, I wanted some information from the concierge, the concierge isn't there . . .

MADELEINE: Naturally.

DETECTIVE: . . . do you know where she is? Do you know if she'll soon be back? Oh, I'm so sorry, please forgive me, I . . . I'd never have knocked on your door, if I'd found the concierge, I wouldn't have dared to trouble you like this . . .

CHOUBERT: The concierge should soon be back, Monsieur. Theoretically she only goes out on Saturday nights. Goes dancing, you know, every Saturday night, since she married her daughter off. And as this is Tuesday night . . .

DETECTIVE: Thank you, Monsieur, thank you very much, I'll be going, Monsieur, I'll wait for her on the landing. You've really been very helpful. Glad to have had the privilege of making your acquaintance, Madame.

MADELEINE: [to CHOUBERT] What a polite young man! Such wonderful manners. Ask him what he wants to know, perhaps you could help him.

CHOUBERT: [to DETECTIVE] Can I help you, Monsieur? Perhaps I can tell you what you want to know?

DETECTIVE: I'm really very sorry to trouble you like this.

MADELEINE: It's no trouble at all.

DETECTIVE: It's really quite a simple matter . . .

MADELEINE: [to CHOUBERT] Why don't you ask him in?

CHOUBERT: [to DETECTIVE] Just step inside a minute, Monsieur.

DETECTIVE: Oh, Monsieur, really, I . . . I . . .

CHOUBERT: My wife would like you to step inside, Monsieur.

MADELEINE: [to DETECTIVE] My husband and I would both like you to step inside, dear Monsieur.

DETECTIVE: [consulting his wristlet watch] I don't really think I've enough time, I'm late already, you see!

MADELEINE: [aside] He's wearing a gold watch!

CHOUBERT: [aside] She's already noticed he's wearing a gold watch!

DETECTIVE: . . . well then, for five minutes, as you insist . . . but I shan't be able to . . . oh well . . . I'll come in if you like, on condition you let me go away again at once . . .

MADELEINE: Don't worry, dear Monsieur, we're not going to keep you here by force, but you can still come in and rest a moment.

DETECTIVE: Thank you, I'm very grateful to you. You're very kind.

[*The* DETECTIVE *takes another step into the room, stops and undoes his overcoat.*]

MADELEINE: [*to* CHOUBERT:] What a lovely brown suit—brand new, too!

CHOUBERT: [*to* MADELEINE] What a wonderful pair of shoes!

MADELEINE: [*to* CHOUBERT] And what lovely fair hair! [*The* DETECTIVE *runs his fingers through his hair.*] Beautiful eyes, such a gentle look. Hasn't he?

CHOUBERT: [*to* MADELEINE] A nice man you feel you can trust. With the face of a child.

MADELEINE: Please don't stand, Monsieur. Do sit down.

CHOUBERT: Take a seat.

[*The* DETECTIVE *takes another step forward. He does not sit down.*]

DETECTIVE: You are Monsieur and Madame Choubert, aren't you?

MADELEINE: Why yes, Monsieur.

DETECTIVE: [*to* CHOUBERT] It seems you're fond of the theatre, Monsieur?

CHOUBERT: Er . . . er . . . yes . . . I take an interest in it.

DETECTIVE: How right you are, Monsieur! I'm very fond of the theatre too, but unfortunately I hardly ever have the time to go.

CHOUBERT: And the sort of plays they put on!

DETECTIVE: [*to* MADELEINE] Monsieur Choubert does, I believe, also support the policy called 'the detachment-system'?

MADELEINE: [*showing little surprise*] Yes, Monsieur, he does.

DETECTIVE: [*to* CHOUBERT] It's an honour for me to share your opinion, Monsieur. [*To both:*] I'm afraid I'm taking your time. I simply wanted to know about the name of the previous tenants of your flat: was it Mallot, with a t at the end, or Mallod with a d? That's all.

CHOUBERT: [*without hesitation*] Mallot, with a t.

DETECTIVE: [*more coldly*] Just as I thought. [*Without speaking, the* DETECTIVE *advances boldly into the room, with* MADELEINE *and* CHOUBERT *on either side, though half a pace behind. The* DETECTIVE *makes for the table, takes hold of one of the two chairs and sits down, while* MADELEINE *and* CHOUBERT *remain standing beside him. The* DETECTIVE *lays his brief case on the table and opens it. He takes a large cigarette-case from his pocket and, without offering any to his hosts, lights one in leisurely fashion, crosses his legs, takes a fresh puff and then:*] So you knew the Mallots?

   [*As he asks this question he looks up, first at* MADELEINE, *then a little longer, at* CHOUBERT.]

CHOUBERT: [*somewhat intrigued*] No. I never knew them.

DETECTIVE: Then how do you know their name ends in a t?

CHOUBERT: [*very surprised*] Why yes, of course, you're right . . . How *do* I know? *How* do I know? . . . How do I *know*? . . . I don't know how I know!

MADELEINE: [*to* CHOUBERT] What's the matter with you? Answer him! When we're on our own you don't swallow your tongue. You talk so fast, you talk too much, such violent language too, and so loud. [*To the* DETECTIVE:] You don't know that side of him. He's a lot brighter than this, in private.

DETECTIVE: I'll make a note of that.

MADELEINE: [*to* DETECTIVE] Still, I'm quite fond of him. After all, he *is* my husband, isn't he? [*To* CHOUBERT:] Oh, come on, now! Did we know the Mallots or not! Say something! Try and remember!

CHOUBERT: [*after struggling silently with his memory for a few moments, while* MADELEINE *gets visibly more irritated and the* DETECTIVE *remains impassive*] I can't remember! Did I know them or not!

DETECTIVE: [*to* MADELEINE] Take his tie off, Madame, perhaps it's worrying him. Then he'll do a bit better.

CHOUBERT: [*to* DETECTIVE] Thank you, Monsieur. [*To* MADELEINE, *who is taking his tie off:*] Thank you, Madeleine.

DETECTIVE: [*to* MADELEINE] The belt too, and his shoe-laces! [MADELEINE *removes them.*]

CHOUBERT: [*to* DETECTIVE] They were a bit too tight, Monsieur, very kind of you.

DETECTIVE: [*to* CHOUBERT] Well, Monsieur?

MADELEINE: [*to* CHOUBERT] Well?

CHOUBERT: It's much easier to breathe. And I feel freer in my movements. But I still can't remember.

DETECTIVE: [*to* CHOUBERT] Come along now, old chap, you're not a child any more.

MADELEINE: [*to* CHOUBERT] Come along, you're not a child. Did you hear what he said? . . . Oh, you're hopeless!

DETECTIVE: [*tipping back on his chair, to* MADELEINE] Will you make me some coffee?

MADELEINE: With pleasure, Monsieur, I'll go and get it ready. Mind you don't tip over, rocking about like that.

DETECTIVE: [*still rocking his chair*] Don't worry, Madeleine. [*With a mysterious smile, to* CHOUBERT:] That is her name, isn't it? [*To* MADELEINE:] Don't worry, Madeleine, I'm used to it . . . Really strong, the coffee, and plenty of sugar!

MADELEINE: Three lumps?

DETECTIVE: Twelve! And a calvados, a large one.

MADELEINE: Very well, Monsieur.

[MADELEINE *leaves the room through the left-hand door. From the wings can be heard the noise of coffee being ground, almost loud enough at the start to drown the voices of* CHOUBERT *and the* DETECTIVE, *and then gradually fading.*]

CHOUBERT: And so, Monsieur, you really are, like me, a firm believer in the 'detachment-system', politically and mystically? And I'm pleased to hear we also have the same tastes in art: I'm sure you accept the principle that the art of drama should be revolutionary.

DETECTIVE: That is not the point we're discussing just now! [*The* DETECTIVE *takes a photo from his pocket and shows it to* CHOUBERT:] See if this photograph can jog your memory. Is this Mallot? [*The* DETECTIVE'S *tone becomes more and more sharp; after a pause:*] Is this Mallot?

[*At the extreme left of the forestage a spotlight should suddenly pick up a large portrait, not noticeable before in the shadows; it roughly resembles the man* CHOUBERT *is describing from the photograph he is looking at in his hand. The characters naturally*] *pay no attention to the illuminated portrait—they appear not to realize it is there—and it disappears again into darkness as soon as the description has been made; it might be better to have an actor, instead of the illuminated portrait, who would stand motionless on the extreme left of the forestage, also looking like the man described; again it might be possible to have both the portrait and the actor, one on each side of the forestage.]*

CHOUBERT: [*after gazing at the photo for some time with great attention and describing the man's face*] It's a man of about fifty . . . yes . . . I see . . . he's got several days' growth of beard . . . and on his chest there's a card with the number 58614 . . . yes, it's 58614 all right . . .

[*The spotlight is cut out; the portrait or the actor is no longer visible on the forestage.*]

DETECTIVE: Is this Mallot? I'm being very patient.

CHOUBERT: [*after a moment's silence*] You know, Monsieur Inspector, I . . .

DETECTIVE: Chief Inspector!

CHOUBERT: I'm sorry, you know, Monsieur Chief Inspector, I can't really tell. Like that, without a tie, collar torn, a face all bruised and swollen, how can I recognize him? . . . And yet it seems to me, yes, it certainly seems it *could* be him . . .

DETECTIVE: When did you know him and what did he talk to you about?

CHOUBERT: [*lowering himself onto a chair*] Forgive me, Monsieur Chief Inspector, I'm terribly tired! . . .

DETECTIVE: My question is: when did you know him and what did he talk to you about?

CHOUBERT: When did I know him? [*He holds his head in his hands.*] What did he *talk* about? What *did* he talk about? *What* did he talk about?

DETECTIVE: Answer!

CHOUBERT: What did he talk to me about? . . . What did he . . . But when on earth did I meet him? . . . When was the first time I saw him? When was the last time?

DETECTIVE: It's not my job to give the answers.

CHOUBERT: Where was it? Where? . . . Where? . . . In the garden? . . . The house I lived in as a child? . . . At school? . . . In the army? . . . On his wedding day? . . . *My* wedding day? . . . Was I his best man? . . . Was *he my* best man? . . . No.

DETECTIVE: You don't want to remember?

CHOUBERT: I can't . . . And yet I do recall . . . some place by the sea, at twilight, it was damp, a long time ago, and dark rocks . . . [*Turning his head to call after* MADELEINE:] Madeleine! Where's that coffee for Monsieur the Chief Inspector!

MADELEINE: [*coming in*] The coffee can grind itself.

CHOUBERT: [*to* MADELEINE] Really, Madeleine, you ought to be seeing to it.

DETECTIVE: [*banging his fist on the table*] All very considerate of you, I'm sure, but it's none of your business. Stick to your own affairs. You were telling me about some place by the sea . . . [CHOUBERT *is silent.*] Did you hear what I said?

MADELEINE: [*overawed by the authoritative tone and gesture of the* DETECTIVE, *in a mixture of fear and admiration, to* CHOUBERT] The gentleman's asking if you heard what he said? Tell him, can't you?

CHOUBERT: Yes, Monsieur.

DETECTIVE: Well? Well?

CHOUBERT: Yes, that's where I must have met him. We must have been very young! . . .

[*It is already obvious, since* MADELEINE *came back on the stage, that she has changed her walk and even her voice; now her old dress falls away and reveals one that is low-cut. She is a different person; her voice, too, has changed; now it is gentle and musical.*]
No, not there! I can't see him there . . .

DETECTIVE: You can't see him there! You can't see him there! Where can it have been then? In the local bistrot? Drunken sot! And he calls himself a married man!

CHOUBERT: When you come to think about it, I suppose, to find Mallot with a t, you must go down, right down . . .

DETECTIVE: Go on down, then.

MADELEINE: [*in her musical voice*] Right down, right down, right down, right down . . .

CHOUBERT: It must be dark down there, won't be able to see anything.

DETECTIVE: I'll show you the way. You've only got to follow my directions: it's not difficult, you just have to let yourself slide.

CHOUBERT: Oh, I'm quite a long way down already.

DETECTIVE: [*harshly*] Not far enough!

MADELEINE: Not far enough, darling, my love, not far enough!
[*She throws her arms round* CHOUBERT, *languorously, almost obscenely; then she is down on her knees before him, forcing him to bend his knees.*] Don't keep your legs so stiff ! Mind you don't slip! the steps are greasy . . . [MADELEINE *has risen to her feet.*] Hold tight to the handrail . . . Down . . . go on down . . . if it's me you want!

[CHOUBERT *is holding on to* MADELEINE's *arm, as if it were a handrail; he looks as though he were going downstairs;* MADELEINE *takes her arm away, but* CHOUBERT *does not notice and goes on clutching an imaginary handrail; he goes on down the stairs towards* MADELEINE. *The expression on his face is lustful; suddenly he stops, holding out an arm and looks at the floor, then all round him.*]

CHOUBERT: This must be it.

DETECTIVE: It'll do, for the moment.

CHOUBERT: Madeleine!

MADELEINE: [*moving back towards the sofa as she intones, musically*]
I am here . . . I am here . . . Further down . . . A stair . . .
A step . . . a stair . . . a step . . . a stair . . . a step . . . a stair . . .
a step . . . a stair . . . Cuckoo . . . Cuckoo . . . [*She lies full-length on the sofa.*] Darling . . .
[CHOUBERT *moves towards her, laughing nervously. For a few moments* MADELEINE, *smiling erotically on the sofa with her arms stretched out to* CHOUBERT, *intones:*]
La, la la la la . . .
[CHOUBERT, *although standing very close to the sofa, has his arms stretched out towards* MADELEINE *as if she were still a long*

*way off; he laughs the same strange laugh and rocks slightly to
and fro; for a few seconds they remain like this, with* MADELEINE
punctuating her singing with provocative laughter, and CHOUBERT
calling her in a thick voice.]

CHOUBERT: Madeleine! Madeleine! I'm coming . . . It's me,
Madeleine! It's me . . . any minute now . . .

DETECTIVE: He's down the first steps all right. Now he must go
right down. He's not doing so badly so far.

[*This erotic scene is broken by the* DETECTIVE'S *interruption;*
MADELEINE *rises to her feet and makes for the back of the stage,
at the same time moving a little nearer the detective; she still
keeps her musical voice for a while, though it gradually becomes
less sensual, but in the end it often takes on the shrewish note it
had before;* CHOUBERT *lets his arms fall to his side, and with an
expressionless face walks with slow mechanical steps towards the*
DETECTIVE.]

You've got to go deeper.

MADELEINE: [*to* CHOUBERT] Deeper, my love, deeper . . . deeper
. . . deeper

CHOUBERT: It's so dark.

DETECTIVE: Think about Mallot and keep your eyes skinned.
Look for Mallot . . .

MADELEINE: [*almost singing*] Look for Mallot, Mallot, Mallot . . .

CHOUBERT: I'm walking through the mud. It's sticking to the
soles of my shoes . . . my feet are so heavy! I'm afraid of
slipping.

DETECTIVE: Don't be afraid. Go on down, till you come to the
bottom, turn right, turn left.

MADELEINE: [*to* CHOUBERT] Down, deeper my darling, darling
deeper down . . .

DETECTIVE: Down, right, left, right, left.

[CHOUBERT *follows the* DETECTIVE'S *directions and goes on
moving like a sleep-walker. Meanwhile* MADELEINE, *her back to
the audience, has thrown her shawl over her shoulders: suddenly she
is all hunched up, and from behind she looks very old. She is
shaken by silent sobbing.*]

DETECTIVE: Straight in front of you . . .

[CHOUBERT *turns to* MADELEINE *and speaks to her. His hands are clasped and his expression is sorrowful.*]

CHOUBERT: Is that you, Madeleine? Is it really you, Madeleine? What a terrible misfortune! How did it happen? How could it happen? We never noticed . . . Poor old lady, poor little faded doll, it's you just the same, but how different you look! When did it happen? Why didn't we stop it? This morning our path was strewn with flowers. The sky was drenched in sunshine. Your laughter rang clear. Our clothes were brand new, and we were surrounded by friends. Nobody had died and you'd never shed a tear. Suddenly it was winter and now ours is an empty road. Where are all the others? In their graves, by the roadside. I want our happiness back again, we've been robbed and despoiled. Oh, when will the light be blue again? Madeleine, you must believe me, I swear it wasn't I who made you old! No . . . I won't have it, I don't believe it, love is always young, love never dies. *I* haven't changed. Neither have you, you're pretending. Oh, but no! I can't deceive myself, you *are* old, so terribly old! Who made you old like that? Old, old, old, old, little old woman, old little doll. Our youth, on the road. Madeleine, little girl, I'll buy you a new dress, primroses, jewels. Your skin will find its bloom again. I want, I love you, I want, oh, please! We don't grow old when we're in love. I love you, grow young again, throw away that mask and look into my eyes. You must laugh, laugh, little girl! To smooth away the wrinkles. Oh, if only we could go singing and skipping and jumping again! I am young. We are young.

[*His back to the audience, he takes* MADELEINE *by the hand, and they both try to sing in a very old voice and skip about. Their voices are cracked and shaken with sobs.*]

CHOUBERT: [*vaguely accompanied by* MADELEINE] Fountains of spring . . . and fresh young leaves . . . The enchanted garden has folded into night, has sunk into the mud . . . Our love in the night, our love in the mud, in the night, in the mud . . .

When our youth has flown, our tears are the pure water of the wells . . . the wells of life, of immortality . . . Do the flowers flower in the mud . . .

DETECTIVE: That's not it, it's not that at all. You're wasting your time, forgetting about Mallot, you stop and hang about, lazy beggar . . . and you're not going in the right direction. If you can't find Mallot in the leaves or the water of the wells, don't stop, keep going. We've no time to lose. While you stand still, he's running God knows where. You, you get soft and sentimental about yourself and stop; it never does to get sentimental; and you must never stop. [*During the* DETECTIVE's *first words* MADELEINE *and* CHOUBERT *have slowly stopped singing. To* MADELEINE, *who has turned round and straightened up:*] As soon as he gets soft, he stops.

CHOUBERT: I won't get soft any more, Monsieur Chief Inspector.

DETECTIVE: That remains to be seen. Go down, turn, down, turn.

[CHOUBERT *has started walking again and* MADELEINE *has again become what she was in the previous scene.*]

CHOUBERT: Have I gone far enough, Monsieur Chief Inspector?

DETECTIVE: Not yet. Go further.

MADELEINE: Cheer up.

CHOUBERT: [*his eyes closed, his arms outstretched*] I've fallen down, but I'm getting up; I've fallen down, but I'm getting up . . .

DETECTIVE: Stay down.

MADELEINE: Stay down, my darling.

DETECTIVE: Look for Mallot, Mallot with a t. Can you see Mallot? Can you see Mallot? . . . Are you getting any nearer?

MADELEINE: Mallot . . . Mallo-o-o-o . . .

CHOUBERT: [*still with his eyes shut*] It doesn't help, however wide I open my eyes . . .

DETECTIVE: I'm not asking you to read with your eyes.

MADELEINE: Go on, let yourself slide, darling.

DETECTIVE: You've got to touch him, catch hold of him, stretch out your arms and grope . . . grope . . . nothing to be frightened of . . .

CHOUBERT: I'm trying . . .

DETECTIVE: He hasn't even got to a thousand metres below sea-level yet.

MADELEINE: Why don't you go further down? Don't be afraid.

CHOUBERT: The tunnel's blocked up.

DETECTIVE: Go straight down where you are, then.

MADELEINE: Go right in, my darling.

DETECTIVE: Can you still talk?

CHOUBERT: The mud's up to my chin.

DETECTIVE: You're not down far enough. Never mind the mud. You're still a long way from Mallot.

MADELEINE: Go right in, darling, go down where it's deepest.

DETECTIVE: Get your chin down, that's it . . . now your mouth . . .

MADELEINE: Your mouth, too. [CHOUBERT *utters stifled grunts.*] Go on, sink right in . . . further, further in, still further . . . [*Grunts from* CHOUBERT.]

DETECTIVE: Now your nose . . .

MADELEINE: Your nose . . .

[*During all this time* CHOUBERT *is miming a descent into the deep, a drowning man.*]

DETECTIVE: His eyes . . .

MADELEINE: He's opened one eye in the mud . . . There's one eyelash showing . . . [*To* CHOUBERT:] Bend your head lower, my love.

DETECTIVE: Why don't you shout louder? He can't hear . . .

MADELEINE: [*to* CHOUBERT, *very loud*] Bend your head lower, my love! . . . Go down! [*To the* DETECTIVE:] He always was hard of hearing.

DETECTIVE: You can still see the top of his ear sticking out.

MADELEINE: [*shouting to* CHOUBERT] Darling! . . . Get your ear under!

CHOUBERT: [*to* MADELEINE] You can see his hair.

MADELEINE: [*to* CHOUBERT] You've still got some hair showing . . . Go right under. Stretch out your arms in the mud, move your fingers about, swim through the deep and find Mallot, whatever you do . . . Down . . . Down . . .

DETECTIVE: You've got to have depth. Of course. Your wife is right. You won't find Mallot until you touch rock bottom.

[*Silence.* CHOUBERT *has really gone very deep. He is advancing with difficulty, his eyes shut, as though on the bed of the ocean.*]

MADELEINE: You can't hear him any more.

DETECTIVE: He's passed the sound barrier.

[*Darkness. For the moment only the characters' voices are heard; they are no longer visible.*]

MADELEINE: Oh, poor darling! I'm frightened for him. I shall never hear it again, that voice I love so well . . .

DETECTIVE: [*harshly to* MADELEINE] It'll come back to us, you'll only make things worse by whining and wailing.

[*Light. Only* MADELEINE *and the* DETECTIVE *are on stage.*]

MADELEINE: You can't see him any more.

DETECTIVE: He's passed the sight barrier.

MADELEINE: He's in danger! He's in danger! I ought never to have agreed to this little game.

DETECTIVE: He'll come back to you, Madeleine, your little treasure, he may be a bit late, but *he'll* be back! *He's* still got a trick or two up his sleeve. He's got the hide of a rhinoceros.

MADELEINE: [*weeping*] I shouldn't have done it. It was wrong of me. When I think of the state he must be in, poor darling . . .

DETECTIVE: [*to* MADELEINE] Be quiet, Madeleine! What are you frightened of, you're with me . . . we're alone, just the two of us, my beauty.

[*He puts his arms absent-mindedly round* MADELEINE, *then takes them away again.*]

MADELEINE: [*weeping*] What have we done! But we had to, didn't we? It's all quite legal?

DETECTIVE: Why yes, of course, there's nothing to fear. He'll come back to you. Cheer up. I'm quite fond of him, too.

MADELEINE: Are you really?

DETECTIVE: He'll come back to us, the long way round . . . He'll live again in us . . . [*Groans coming from the wings.*] You hear . . . It's him breathing . . .

MADELEINE: Yes, that breathing I love so well.

[*Darkness. Light.* CHOUBERT *passes right across the stage. The other two characters are no longer there.*]

CHOUBERT: I can see . . . I can see . . .

[*His words are lost in groans. He goes out on the right, while* MADELEINE *and the* DETECTIVE *come back from the left. They are transformed. The actors who play the following scene have become two different characters.*]

MADELEINE: You're a despicable creature! You've spent a whole lifetime humiliating and torturing me. Morally you've disfigured me. You've made me old before my time. You've destroyed me. I've finished with you.

DETECTIVE: And what do you think you're going to do?

MADELEINE: Kill myself, take poison.

DETECTIVE: You're free to do as you like, I'll not stop you.

MADELEINE: You'd be only too pleased to get rid of me! You'd *love* to be rid of me, wouldn't you? I know you would!

DETECTIVE: I don't want to get rid of you at *any* price! But I can quite easily get along without you. You and your compl ining. It's just you're so boring. You know nothing about life, you bore everyone stiff.

MADELEINE: [*sobbing*] Brute!

DETECTIVE: Don't cry, it makes you even uglier than usual! . . .

[CHOUBERT *has appeared again, and watches the scene from afar, without a word, wringing his hands, as though powerless to intervene; at the most he can be heard muttering: 'Father, mother, father, mother . . .'*]

MADELEINE: [*beside herself*] Now you've gone too far. I can't bear it. [*She takes from her bosom a small bottle she then carries to her lips.*]

DETECTIVE: You're mad, you're not going to do that! Stop it!

[*The* DETECTIVE *goes to* MADELEINE *and takes her by the arm to prevent her swallowing the poison; then suddenly, as the expression on his face changes, it is he who forces her to drink.*

CHOUBERT *utters a cry. Black-out. Lights again. He is clene on the stage.*]

CHOUBERT: I am eight years old and it's evening. My mother's holding me by the hand, in the rue Blomet after the bombing. We're walking along by the ruins. I'm frightened. My mother's hand is shaking in mine. There are shadowy figures looming in the gaps in the walls. The only light in the darkness comes from their eyes.

[MADELEINE *appears silently. She goes towards* CHOUBERT. *It's his mother.*]

DETECTIVE: [*appearing at the other side of the stage and advancing with very slow steps*] Those shadowy figures, look, perhaps one of them is Mallot . . .

CHOUBERT: The light's gone from their eyes. Everything's returned to night, except for a skylight in the distance. It's so dark I can't see my mother any more. Her hand has melted away. I can hear her voice.

DETECTIVE: She must be talking about Mallot.

CHOUBERT: Sadly, very sadly she's saying: I'm going to leave you, and you'll have many a tear to shed, my child, my little lamb . . .

MADELEINE: [*with great tenderness in her voice*] My child, my little lamb . . .

CHOUBERT: I shall be alone in the dark, in the mud . . .

MADELEINE: My poor child, in the dark, in the mud, all alone, little lamb . . .

CHOUBERT: There's only her voice, a whisper to guide me. She's saying . . .

MADELEINE: You must learn to forgive, my child, that's the hardest of all . . .

CHOUBERT: That's the hardest of all.

MADELEINE: That's the hardest of all.

CHOUBERT: And now she's saying . . .

MADELEINE: . . . The time for tears will come, the time for repentance and remorse, you must be good, you'll suffer for it if you're not and you never learn to forgive. When you see him, obey him, kiss him and forgive him.

[MADELEINE *goes out in silence.*

CHOUBERT *is in front of the* DETECTIVE, *who is sitting at the table facing the audience and holding his head in his hands, staying quite still.*]

CHOUBERT: Now the voice is silent. [CHOUBERT *addresses the* DETECTIVE:] Father, we never understood each other . . . Can you still hear me? I'll be obedient; forgive us as we forgave you . . . Let me see your face! [*The* DETECTIVE *does not move.*] You were hard, but perhaps you weren't too unkind. Perhaps it's not your fault. It's not you I hated. It was your selfishness and your violence. I had no pity for your frailties. You used to hit me. But I was stronger than you. My contempt hit you much harder. That was what killed you. Wasn't it? Listen . . . I had to avenge my mother . . . I *had* to . . . What *was* my duty? . . . Did I really *have* to? . . . She forgave you, but I went on and carried out *her* revenge myself . . . What's the good of taking vengeance? It's always the avenger who suffers . . . Do you hear me? Uncover your face. Give me your hand. We could have been good pals. I was far more unkind than you. You had your middle-class ways, but what did that matter? I was wrong to despise you. I'm no better than you are. What right had I to punish you? [*The* DETECTIVE *is still motionless.*] Let's make it up! Let's be friends! Give me your hand! That's it, come with me and we'll go and find some of the boys! We'll all have a drink together. Look at me, look! I take after you. You don't want to . . . If you would look at me, you'd see how alike we are. I've all the same faults as you. [*Silence. The* DETECTIVE's *position does not change.*] Who will have mercy on me, I who have been unmerciful! Even if you did forgive me, I could never forgive myself !

[*While the* DETECTIVE's *position remains unchanged, his recorded voice is heard coming from the opposite corner of the stage; during the ensuing monologue* CHOUBERT *stands quite still, arms hanging at his sides; his face expresses no emotion, but his body is occasionally shaken by shuddering despair.*][1]

---

1 AUTHOR'S NOTE: During the actual performance the DETECTIVE raised his head and spoke directly. This seems the better solution.

DETECTIVE'S VOICE:[1] My boy, I was a travelling salesman. My job sent me roving all over the globe. Unfortunately I always had to spend October to March in the northern hemisphere, and April to September in the southern, with the result that in my life it was winter all the time. My pay was wretched, my clothes were poor and my health was bad. I lived in a perpetual state of rage. My enemies grew richer and richer, and more and more powerful. Those who helped me went bankrupt and then they died, carried off, one after the other, by disreputable diseases or preposterous little accidents. I met nothing but disappointment. The good I did turned into evil, but the evil done to me never turned into good. Later I was a soldier, I was compelled, ordered to join in the massacre of tens of thousands of enemy soldiers, of whole communities of old men, women and children. Then the town where I was born, with all its suburbs, was utterly destroyed. In peacetime the misery went on, and I had a horror of mankind. I planned all kinds of horrible revenge. I loathed the earth, the sun and its satellites. I longed to go into voluntary exile, to another universe. But there *is* no other.

CHOUBERT: [*in the same attitude*] He doesn't want to look at me . . . to speak to me . . .

DETECTIVE'S VOICE:[1] [*while the* DETECTIVE *himself is still in the same position*] You were born, my son, just when I was about to blow our planet up. It was only your arrival that saved it. At least, it was you who stopped me from killing mankind in my heart. You reconciled me to the human race and bound me irrevocably to the history, the crimes and hopes, despairs and disasters of all men. I trembled for their fate . . . and for yours.

CHOUBERT: [*he and the* DETECTIVE *as before*] So I shall never know . . .

DETECTIVE'S VOICE:[1] Yes, you had hardly emerged from the void when I began to feel I'd lost my weapons; I was gasping with joy and sorrow, my stony heart had turned into a sponge,

1 Or the DETECTIVE himself.

a rag; my head was spinning with unspeakable remorse to think I'd not wanted a family and had tried to stop you coming into the world. You might never have been, never have been! Only to think of it now, I still get a tremendous feeling of panic; heart-rending regret, too, for all those thousands of children who might have been born and who haven't, for those countless faces never to be caressed, those little hands that no father will ever hold in his, those lips that will never know prattling. I should have liked to fill the emptiness with life. I tried to imagine all those little beings who so nearly came into existence, I wanted to create them in my mind, so that I could at least weep for them, as I weep for those who are really dead.

CHOUBERT: [*both he and the* DETECTIVE, *still in the same positions*] He'll never open his mouth!

DETECTIVE'S VOICE:[1] Yet, at the same time, I was overcome with delirious joy, for you, dear child, existed, you, a flickering star in an ocean of darkness, an island of being surrounded by nothing, and your existence cancelled out the void. I wept as my lips brushed your eyes: 'Oh God, oh God!' I sighed. I was grateful to God, because if the creation had never been, if the universe had never had a history, century after century, then *you* would never have been, my son, and all the history of the world really led up to you. You would never have been here, were it not for that endless chain of cause and effect, not forgetting all the floods, the wars and revolutions, and every social, geological and cosmic catastrophe that ever was: for everything in the universe is the result of a whole system of causation, not excepting you, my child. I was grateful to God for all my misery and for all the misery of centuries, for all the sorrow and all the joy, for the humiliation, for the horror and the anguish, for the great sadness, since at the end there was your birth, which justified and redeemed in my eyes all the disasters of History. I had forgiven the world, for love of you. Everything was saved, because now nothing could ever

1 Or the DETECTIVE himself.

wipe out the fact of your birth into the living universe. Even when you are no more, I told myself, nothing can alter the fact that you *have been*. You were here, for ever inscribed in the archives of the universe, firmly fixed in the eternal memory of God.

CHOUBERT: [*both he and the* DETECTIVE *still in the same positions*] He'll never, never, never say . . .

DETECTIVE'S VOICE:[1] [*change of tone*] And you . . . The more proud I was of you, the more I loved you, the more you despised me, accused me of every crime, some I had committed, others I had not. Then there was your mother, poor soul. But who can tell what passed between us, whether it was her fault, or my fault, her fault or my fault . . .

CHOUBERT: [*both as before*] He'll never speak again, and it's all my fault, my fault! . . .

DETECTIVE'S VOICE:[1] You can reject me and blush for me and insult my memory as much as you like. I'll not blame you. I'm no longer capable of hate. I can't help forgiving. I owe you more than you owe me. I wouldn't want you to suffer, I want you to stop feeling guilty. Forget what you consider to be my faults.

CHOUBERT: Father, why don't you speak, why don't you answer me! . . . How sad to think that never, never again I shall hear your voice . . . Never, never, never, never . . . And I shall never know . . .

DETECTIVE: [*abruptly, as he stands up, to* CHOUBERT] In this country a father's heart's as soft as a mother's. Moaning won't do any good. What's your personal life to do with us? You stick to Mallot! Keep on his tracks. Don't think about anything else. There's nothing in the whole business of any interest, except Mallot. Forget the rest of it, I tell you.

CHOUBERT: Monsieur Chief Inspector, you see, I really would have liked to know . . . Were they . . . After all they were my parents . . .

DETECTIVE: Oh, you and your complexes! Don't start worrying

1 Or the DETECTIVE himself.

us with them! I don't give a damn for your daddy and your
mummy and your filial affection! . . . That's not what I'm
paid for. Get back on the road.

CHOUBERT: Have I really still got to go down, Monsieur Chief
Inspector? . . .

[*He searches blindly with his foot.*]

DETECTIVE: You must describe everything you see!

CHOUBERT: [*advancing hesitantly, like a blind man*] . . . A step to
the right . . . Step to the left . . . to the left . . . left . . .

DETECTIVE: [*to* MADELEINE, *who comes back from the right*] Mind
the steps, Madame . . .

MADELEINE: Thank you so much, I could have fallen . . .

[*The* DETECTIVE *and* MADELEINE *have become theatre-goers.*]

DETECTIVE: [*hurrying towards* MADELEINE] Better take my arm . . .

[*The* DETECTIVE *and* MADELEINE *are finding their seats;*
CHOUBERT *disappears for a moment in the semi-darkness, after
walking away with the same hesitant step; he is to reappear in a
moment at the other side on a platform or small stage.*]

DETECTIVE: [*to* MADELEINE] Shall we find our seats and sit down?
It's going to begin. Every evening he shows himself off like
this.

MADELEINE: I'm glad you booked the tickets.

DETECTIVE: Here we are.

[*He sets the two chairs down beside each other.*]

MADELEINE: Thank you, how kind. Are they good seats? Are
they the best? Can we see everything? And hear everything?
Have you any opera-glasses?

[CHOUBERT *has come into full view on the little stage, groping
his way.*]

DETECTIVE: There he is . . .

MADELEINE: Oh, he makes quite an impression, quite a good
actor! Is he really blind?

DETECTIVE: No way of knowing. But you'd think so.

MADELEINE: Poor man! They really ought to have given him a
pair of white sticks, a small one, like a policeman's, so he
could direct the traffic all by himself, and a larger one, like a

blind man's . . . [*To the* DETECTIVE:] Must I remove my hat? Oh no, I don't think so, do you? It's not in anyone's way. I'm not so tall as all that.

DETECTIVE: He's talking, be quiet, we can't hear him.

MADELEINE: [*to* DETECTIVE] Perhaps that's because he's deaf as well . . .

CHOUBERT: [*on the platform*] Where am I?

MADELEINE: [*to* DETECTIVE] Where is he?

DETECTIVE: [*to* MADELEINE] Don't be so impatient. He's going to tell you. It's all in his part.

CHOUBERT: . . . sorts of streets . . . sorts of roads . . . sorts of lakes . . . sorts of people . . . sorts of nights . . . sorts of skies . . . a sort of world . . .

MADELEINE: [*to* DETECTIVE] What's he say? . . . sorts of what?

DETECTIVE: [*to* MADELEINE] All sorts of sorts . . .

MADELEINE: [*loudly to* CHOUBERT] Louder!

DETECTIVE: [*to* MADELEINE] Be quiet, can't you? That's not allowed.

CHOUBERT: . . . Shades waking to life . . .

MADELEINE: [*to* DETECTIVE] What! . . . Is that all we're good for, just to pay up and applaud? [*Still louder, to* CHOUBERT:] Louder!

CHOUBERT: [*still acting*] . . . nostalgia, shreds and fragments of a universe . . .

MADELEINE: [*to* DETECTIVE] What does that mean?

DETECTIVE: [*to* MADELEINE] He said: fragments of a universe . . .

CHOUBERT: [*as before*] A yawning pit . . .

DETECTIVE: [*whispering in* MADELEINE's *ear*] A yawning pit . . .

MADELEINE: [*to* DETECTIVE] He's not normal. He must be ill. He ought to keep his feet on the ground.

DETECTIVE: [*to* MADELEINE] He can't, he's underground.

MADELEINE: [*to* DETECTIVE] Oh yes! That's true! [*Admiringly*] You're a wonderful man, so clever at understanding things!

CHOUBERT: [*still acting*] Resign myself . . . resign myself . . . The light is dark . . . the stars are dim . . . I'm suffering from an unknown disease . . .

MADELEINE: [*to* DETECTIVE] What's the name of the actor playing this part?

DETECTIVE: Choubert.

MADELEINE: [*to* DETECTIVE] Not the composer, I hope!

DETECTIVE: [*to* MADELEINE] No fear.

MADELEINE: [*very loud, to* CHOUBERT] Speak up!

CHOUBERT: My face is wet with tears. Where has beauty gone? And goodness? And love? I've lost my memory . . .

MADELEINE: This is a fine time! Just when there isn't a prompter!

CHOUBERT: [*in a tone of great despair*] My toys . . . in pieces . . . My toys are broken . . . The toys I had as a child . . .

MADELEINE: So childish!

DETECTIVE: [*to* MADELEINE] Quite a pertinent remark!

CHOUBERT: [*with the same intensity of despair*] I am old . . . I am old . . .

MADELEINE: Doesn't look as old as that. He's exaggerating. He wants us to pity him.

CHOUBERT: In days gone by . . . gone by . . .

MADELEINE: What's happening now?

DETECTIVE: [*to* MADELEINE] He's remembering his past, I suppose, dear lady.

MADELEINE: If we all started reminiscing, where would it end . . . We'd all have something to say. We take good care not to. We're too shy, too modest.

CHOUBERT: . . . In days gone by . . . A great wind arose . . . [*He groans loudly.*]

MADELEINE: He's crying . . .

DETECTIVE: [*to* MADELEINE] He's imitating the sound of the wind . . . through the forest.

CHOUBERT: [*continuing as before*] The wind shakes the forests, the lightning rends the thick gloom, and there on the horizon, behind the storm, a gigantic curtain of darkness is heavily lifting . . .

MADELEINE: What's that? What's that?

CHOUBERT: [*as before*] . . . and there, appearing in the distance,

gleaming through the shadows, still as a dream in the midst of
the storm, a magic city . . .

MADELEINE: [to DETECTIVE] A what?

DETECTIVE: The city! The city!

MADELEINE: I see.

CHOUBERT: [as before] . . . or a magic garden, a bubbling spring
and fountains and flowers of fire in the night . . .

MADELEINE: And I bet you he thinks he's a poet! A lot of bad
parnassian-symbolic-surrealism.

CHOUBERT: [as before] . . . a palace of icy flames, glowing statues
and incandescent seas, continents blazing in the night, in
oceans of snow!

MADELEINE: He's an old ham! It's ridiculous! Unthinkable!
He's a liar!

DETECTIVE: [shouting to CHOUBERT, half of him becoming the
DETECTIVE again, though the other half is still an astonished theatre-
goer] Can you see his dark shadow outlined against the light?
Or is it a shining silhouette outlined against the dark?

CHOUBERT: The fire has lost its brightness, the palace its brilliance,
it's getting darker.

DETECTIVE: [to CHOUBERT] At least you can say what you feel! . . .
What are your feelings? Tell us!

MADELEINE: [to DETECTIVE] My dear, we'd far better spend the
rest of the evening at a cabaret . . .

CHOUBERT: [as before] . . . Joy . . . and pain . . . tearing you . . .
healing you . . . Fullness . . . And emptiness . . . Hopeless
hope. I feel strong, I feel weak, I feel ill, I feel well, but I feel,
above all, I feel myself, still, I feel myself . . .

MADELEINE: [to DETECTIVE] All he does is contradict himself.

DETECTIVE: [to CHOUBERT] And then? And then? [To MADELEINE:]
One minute, dear lady, forgive me . . .

CHOUBERT: [with a great shout] Is it all going out? It is going out.
The night's all around me. Only one butterfly of light painfully
rising . . .

MADELEINE: [to DETECTIVE] My dear man, he's a fraud . . .

CHOUBERT: One last spark . . .

MADELEINE: [*applauding as the curtains of the small stage close*] So dull and ordinary. It could have been so much more amusing . . . or at least instructive, couldn't it, but I suppose . . .

DETECTIVE: [*to* CHOUBERT *who is at this moment hidden by the curtains*] No, No! You've got to start walking. [*To* MADELEINE:] He's on the wrong road. We must put him back on the right one.

MADELEINE: We'll give him another round.

[*They clap.* CHOUBERT'S *head reappears for an instant between the curtains of the small stage, then disappears again.*]

DETECTIVE: Choubert, Choubert, Choubert. You must realize Mallot's got to be found again. It's a question of life and death. It's your duty. The fate of all mankind depends on you. It's not as difficult as that, you've only got to remember. Remember and then everything will come clear again . . . [*To* MADELEINE:] He'd gone too far down. He's got to come up again . . . A little . . . in our estimation.

MADELEINE: [*timidly, to the* DETECTIVE] He felt all right, though.

DETECTIVE: [*to* CHOUBERT] Are you there? Are you there?

[*The small stage has vanished.* CHOUBERT *appears again at another spot.*]

CHOUBERT: I'm turning my memories over.

DETECTIVE: Do it systematically, then.

MADELEINE: [*to* CHOUBERT] Turn them over systematically. Listen and do what you're told.

CHOUBERT: I'm back on the surface again.

DETECTIVE: That's good, old chap, that's good . . .

CHOUBERT: [*to* MADELEINE] Do *you* remember?

DETECTIVE: [*to* MADELEINE] You see, he's getting on better already.

CHOUBERT: Honfleur . . . How blue the sea is . . . No . . . At Mont Saint-Michel . . . No . . . Dieppe . . . No, I've never been there . . . at Cannes . . . not there either.

DETECTIVE: Trouville, Deauville . . .

CHOUBERT: Never been there either.

MADELEINE: He's never been there either.

CHOUBERT: Collioure. Architects once built a temple there on the waving sea.

MADELEINE: He's raving!

DETECTIVE: [*to* MADELEINE] Stop this silly playing with words!

CHOUBERT: No sign of Montbéliard . . .

DETECTIVE: It's true, Montbéliard, that was his nickname. And you pretended not to know him!

MADELEINE: [*to* CHOUBERT] You see!

CHOUBERT: [*very astonished*] Why yes, good Lord, yes . . . It's true . . . it's funny, it's true.

DETECTIVE: Look somewhere else. Come on, now, quick, the towns . . .

CHOUBERT: Paris, Palermo, Pisa, Berlin, New York . . .

DETECTIVE: The mountains and the gorges . . .

MADELEINE: Mountains, well there ought to be plenty of them about . . .

DETECTIVE: Why not in the Andes, in the Andes . . . have you been there?

MADELEINE: [*to* DETECTIVE] Actually, Monsieur, he hasn't . . .

CHOUBERT: No, but I know enough geography to . . .

DETECTIVE: You mustn't invent. You must find him again. Come on, old chap, just a little effort . . .

CHOUBERT: [*making a painful effort*] Mallot with a t, Montbéliard with a d, with a t, with a d . . .

[*If the producer so desires, the same character who appeared before can be spotlighted again at the other side of the stage: he still has his number and, in addition, an alpenstock, a rope or a pair of skis. Once again he vanishes after a few moments.*]

CHOUBERT: Swept along by the surface currents, I'm crossing the ocean. Landing in Spain. Making for France. The customs officials are touching their caps. Narbonne, Marseille, Aix, the watery grave. Arles, Avignon, with its popes, its mules and its palaces. In the distance, Mont Blanc.

MADELEINE: [*who is gradually beginning to object rather slyly to* CHOUBERT's *latest itinerary, to* DETECTIVE] The forest's between you.

DETECTIVE: Go on just the same.

CHOUBERT: I'm going through the trees. How fresh it is! Is it evening?

MADELEINE: The forest is dense . . .

DETECTIVE: Don't be afraid.

CHOUBERT: I can hear the bubbling of the springs. Wings are brushing my face. Grass up to my waist. The tracks have finished. Madeleine, give me your hand.

DETECTIVE: [to MADELEINE] Whatever you do, don't give him your hand.

MADELEINE: [to CHOUBERT] Not my hand, he won't let me.

DETECTIVE: [to CHOUBERT] You can find your own way through. Use your eyes! Look above you!

CHOUBERT: The sun's shining between the trees. Blue light. I'm advancing quickly, the branches are moving aside. Twenty feet away the woodcutters are working and whistling . . .

MADELEINE: They may not be *real* woodcutters . . .

DETECTIVE: [to MADELEINE] Quiet!

CHOUBERT: There's a bright light ahead. I'm coming out of the forest . . . into a pink village.

MADELEINE: My favourite colour . . .

CHOUBERT: Low cottages.

DETECTIVE: Can you see anyone?

CHOUBERT: It's too early. The shutters are closed. The square's empty. A fountain and a statue. I'm running, and the echo of my clogs . . .

MADELEINE: [shrugging her shoulders] His clogs!

DETECTIVE: Keep going. You're nearly there . . . Keep moving.

MADELEINE: Moving, always moving, moving forward.

CHOUBERT: The land is flat, but gently rising. Another stretch and I'm at the foot of the mountain.

DETECTIVE: Up you go.

CHOUBERT: I'm climbing a steep path, have to hang on. I've left the forest behind me. The village is right down below. I'm getting higher. A lake on the right.

DETECTIVE: Go on up.

MADELEINE: He wants you to go on if you can. If you can!

CHOUBERT: It's so steep! Thorns and stones. The lake's behind me. I can see the Mediterranean.

DETECTIVE: Go on up, up.

MADELEINE: Up further, that's what he says.

CHOUBERT: A fox, last of the animals. A blind owl. Not another bird in sight. No more springs . . . No more tracks . . . No more echo. I'm sweeping the horizon.

DETECTIVE: Can you see *him*?

CHOUBERT: It's an empty waste.

DETECTIVE: Higher. Go on up.

MADELEINE: Up further, then, as it can't be helped.

CHOUBERT: I'm clinging to the stones, I'm slipping and clutching at thorns, crawling on all fours . . . Oh, the altitude's too much for me . . . Why do I always have to climb mountains . . . Why am I always the one who's made to do the impossible . . .

MADELEINE: [*to* DETECTIVE] The impossible . . . He said it himself. [*To* CHOUBERT:] You ought to be ashamed.

CHOUBERT: I'm thirsty, I'm hot, I'm sweating.

DETECTIVE: Don't stop now to wipe your brow. You can do that later. Later. Go on up.

CHOUBERT: . . . So tired . . .

MADELEINE: Already! [*To* DETECTIVE:] Believe me, Monsieur Chief Inspector, it doesn't surprise me. He's quite incapable.

DETECTIVE: [*to* CHOUBERT] Lazy devil!

MADELEINE: [*to* DETECTIVE] He's always been lazy. Never gets anywhere.

CHOUBERT: Not a scrap of shade. The sun's enormous. A furnace. I'm stifling. Roasting.

DETECTIVE: You can't be far away now, you see, you're getting warm.

MADELEINE: [*unheard by the* DETECTIVE] I could send someone else in your place . . .

CHOUBERT: Another mountain ahead of me. A wall without a crack. I'm out of breath.

DETECTIVE: Higher, higher.

MADELEINE: [*very fast, n w to the* DETECTIVE, *now to* CHOUBERT] Higher. He's out of breath. Higher. He mustn't rise too high above us. You'd better come down. Up higher. Down lower. Up higher.

DETECTIVE: Go on, higher.

MADELEINE: Up. Down.

CHOUBERT: My hands are bleeding.

MADELEINE: [*to* CHOUBERT] Up. Down.

DETECTIVE: Hang on. Climb.

CHOUBERT: [*quite still, continuing his ascent*] It's hard to be alone in the world! If only I'd had a son!

MADELEINE: I'd rather have had a girl. Boys are so ungrateful!

DETECTIVE: [*tapping his foot*] Kindly keep these observations for a different occasion. [*To* CHOUBERT:] Go on up, don't waste time.

MADELEINE: Up. Down.

CHOUBERT: After all, I'm only a man.

DETECTIVE: You must be a man to the bitter end.

MADELEINE: [*to* CHOUBERT] Be a man to the bitter end.

CHOUBERT: No-o-o! . . . No! . . . I can't lift my knees again. I can't bear it!

DETECTIVE: Come on now, one last effort.

MADELEINE: One last effort. Do try. No, don't. Do try.

CHOUBERT: I've done it, I've done it. I'm here. At the top! . . . You can see right through the sky, but there's no sign of Montbéliard.[1]

MADELEINE: [*to* DETECTIVE] He's going to escape us, Monsieur Chief Inspector.

DETECTIVE: [*not hearing* MADELEINE, *to* CHOUBERT] Look for him, look.

MADELEINE: [*to* CHOUBERT] Look, stop looking, look, stop looking. [*To* DETECTIVE:] He's going to escape you.

---

1 In Jacques Mauclair's production CHOUBERT's ascent was made in the following manner: he first crawled under the table, climbed on to it and then stood on a chair that he had placed on the table. He started walking when he said: 'I'm going through the trees' . . .

CHOUBERT: There's no more . . . No more . . . No more . . .

MADELEINE: No more what?

CHOUBERT: No more towns, or woods, or valleys, or sea, or sky. I'm alone.

MADELEINE: If you were down here, there'd be two of us.

DETECTIVE: What's he talking about? What does he mean? And what about Mallot and Montbéliard!

CHOUBERT: I can run without walking.

MADELEINE: He's going to take off . . . Choubert! Do you hear . . .

CHOUBERT: I'm alone. I've lost my footing. I'm not dizzy . . . I'm not afraid to die any more.

DETECTIVE: I couldn't care less about that.

MADELEINE: Think about us. It's not good to be alone. You can't leave us . . . Have pity, pity! [*She is a beggarwoman.*] I've no bread for my children. I've got four children. My husband's in prison. I'm just out of hospital. I'm sure you've a kind heart, Sir . . . [*To* DETECTIVE:] What I've had to put up with, with him! . . . You understand me now, Monsieur Chief Inspector?

DETECTIVE: [*to* CHOUBERT] Remember the solidarity of the human race. [*Aside*] I've driven him too far. Now he's getting away from us. [*Shouting*] Choubert, Choubert, Choubert . . . My dear old chap, we've both got on the wrong track.

MADELEINE: [*to* DETECTIVE] I told you so.

DETECTIVE: [*slapping* MADELEINE's *face*] I didn't ask your opinion.

MADELEINE: [*to* DETECTIVE] I'm sorry, Monsieur Chief Inspector.

DETECTIVE: [*to* CHOUBERT] It's your duty to look for Mallot, your duty to look for Mallot, you're not betraying your friends, Mallot, Montbéliard, Mallot, Montbéliard! Why don't you look, look! Can't you see you're not looking! What can you see? . . . Look in front of you. Answer me, do you hear? Answer . . .

MADELEINE: Why don't you answer?

[*To persuade* CHOUBERT *to come down,* MADELEINE *and the* DETECTIVE *draw a picture of all the advantages of everyday life in society.* MADELEINE *and the* DETECTIVE *become more and more grotesque, until they are almost clowning.*]

CHOUBERT: It's a morning in June. The air I breathe is lighter than air. *I* am lighter than air. The sun's melting into light that's mightier than the sun. I can float through solid objects. All forms have disappeared. I'm going up . . . and up . . . shimmering light . . . and up . . .

MADELEINE: He's getting away! . . . I told you so, Monsieur Chief Inspector, I told you he would . . . I won't have it, I won't have it. [*Speaking in* CHOUBERT's *direction:*] You might at least take me with you.

DETECTIVE: [*to* CHOUBERT] Hey! . . . You wouldn't do that to me . . . Eh? Would you? . . . Bastard . . .

CHOUBERT: [*without mime, talking to himself*] Can I . . . go through . . . over the top . . . can I . . . jump . . . one step . . . lightly . . . one . . .

DETECTIVE: [*military march*] One, two, One, two . . . I taught you your arms drill, you were a quartermaster's clerk . . . Don't pretend you can't hear me, you're not the type to desert . . . and don't be cheeky to your sergeant-major! . . . Discipline! [*A bugle sounds.*] . . . The country that bore you has need of you.

MADELEINE: [*to* CHOUBERT] You're all I've got to live for.

DETECTIVE: [*to* CHOUBERT] You've got your life, your career ahead of you! You'll be rich, happy and stupid, a chargé d'affaires! Here's your appointment! [*He holds out a paper that* CHOUBERT *ignores; this is really the time for* MADELEINE *and the* DETECTIVE *to give their show. To* MADELEINE:] There's still hope, all the time we can keep him from flying away . . .

MADELEINE: [*to the still motionless* CHOUBERT] Here's gold for you, and fruit . . .

DETECTIVE: The heads of your enemies will be served to you on a plate.

MADELEINE: You can take what revenge you like, be as sadistic as you want!

DETECTIVE: I'll make you archbishop.

MADELEINE: Pope!

DETECTIVE: If you like. [*To* MADELEINE:] Perhaps we wouldn't
be able to . . . [*To* CHOUBERT:] If you like, you can start life
afresh, learn to walk again . . . fulfil your ambitions.

CHOUBERT: [*neither seeing nor hearing the others*] I'm gliding over a
rocky surface, ever so high. I can fly!

[*The* DETECTIVE *and* MADELEINE *hold on to* CHOUBERT.]

MADELEINE: Quick! . . . He needs some more ballast . . .

DETECTIVE: [*to* MADELEINE] Mind your own business . . .

MADELEINE: [*to* DETECTIVE] You're somewhat to blame for this,
too, Monsieur Chief Inspector . . .

DETECTIVE: [*to* MADELEINE] No, it's you. I wasn't properly
backed up. You didn't understand. I was given a partner who's
nothing but a clumsy little fool . . .

[MADELEINE *weeps.*]

MADELEINE: Oh! Monsieur Chief Inspector!

DETECTIVE: [*to* MADELEINE] A little fool! . . . Yes, a fool . . .
fool . . . fool . . . [*Turning abruptly to* CHOUBERT:] It's lovely
in our valleys in the spring, the winter's mild and it never rains
in summer . . .

MADELEINE: [*to* DETECTIVE, *snivelling*] I did my best, Monsieur
Chief Inspector. I did all I could.

DETECTIVE: [*to* MADELEINE] Silly little fool!

MADELEINE: You're quite right, Monsieur Chief Inspector.

DETECTIVE: [*to* CHOUBERT *in a desperate voice*] And what of the
huge reward for the man who finds Mallot? Even if you lose
your honour, you realize you'll still have the money, the
uniform and the honours that go with them! . . . What more do
you want!

CHOUBERT: I can fly.

MADELEINE AND DETECTIVE: [*clinging onto* CHOUBERT] No! No!
No! Don't do that!

CHOUBERT: I'm bathing in the light. [*Total darkness on the stage.*]
The light is seeping through me. I'm so surprised to be, surprised to be, surprised to be . . .

TRIUMPHANT VOICE OF DETECTIVE: He'll never pass the surprise
barrier.

VOICE OF MADELEINE: Be careful, Choubert . . . remember how giddy you get.

VOICE OF CHOUBERT: I am light! I'm flying!

VOICE OF MADELEINE: Well, why don't you fall and put yourself out!

VOICE OF DETECTIVE: That's the stuff, Madeleine!

VOICE OF CHOUBERT: [*suddenly in distress*] Oh! . . . I don't dare . . . I feel ill . . . I'm going to jump! . . .

    [CHOUBERT *is heard groaning. The stage is lit again.* CHOUBERT *is sprawling in a large waste-paper basket, with* MADELEINE *and the* DETECTIVE *standing over him. A new character, a* LADY, *who takes no notice at all of what is going on, is sitting on the left, near the wall, on a chair.*]

DETECTIVE: [*to* CHOUBERT] Well, my lad?

CHOUBERT: Where am I?

DETECTIVE: Have a look round, fathead!

CHOUBERT: What! Were you still here, Monsieur Chief Inspector? How did you manage to find a way into my memories?

DETECTIVE: I followed you . . . every step. Luckily!

MADELEINE: Oh yes! It's lucky you did!

DETECTIVE: [*to* CHOUBERT] Right! On your feet! [*He pulls him up by his ears.*] If I'd not been here . . . If I'd not pulled you back . . . You're so light-headed you're practically disembodied, you've no memory, you forget everything, forget yourself, forget your duty. That's your great fault. You're either too heavy or too light.

MADELEINE: I think it's rather that he's too heavy.

DETECTIVE: [*to* MADELEINE] I don't like being contradicted! [*To* CHOUBERT:] I'll cure you all right . . . That's what I'm here for.

CHOUBERT: And *I* thought I'd reached the top. Higher even.

    [CHOUBERT'S *behaviour gets more and more babyish.*]

DETECTIVE: That's not what you were asked to do!

CHOUBERT: Oh . . . I took the wrong road . . . I'm cold . . . My feet are soaking . . . I've shivers down my spine. Have you got a nice dry sweater?

MADELEINE: Ah! He's got shivers down his spine, has he! . . .

DETECTIVE: [*to* MADELEINE] It's only because he wants to get his own back.

CHOUBERT: [*like a child excusing himself*] It's not my fault . . . I looked everywhere. I couldn't find him . . . It's not my fault . . . . You were watching me, you saw . . . I wasn't cheating.

MADELEINE: [*to* DETECTIVE] He's weak in the head. How could I ever have married such a man! He made far more impression when he was younger! [*To* CHOUBERT:] Do you hear? [*To* DETECTIVE:] He's an old fox, Monsieur Chief Inspector, I told you he was, and a sly one too! . . . But he's much too feeble . . . He wants fattening up, put some stuffing into him . . .

DETECTIVE: [*to* CHOUBERT] You're weak in the head! How could she ever have married such a man! You made far more impression when you were younger! Do you hear? You're an old fox, I told you you were, and a sly one too! . . . But you're much too feeble, and you need some stuffing . . .

CHOUBERT: [*to* DETECTIVE] Madeleine just said exactly the same. Monsieur Chief Inspector, you're a copy-cat!

MADELEINE: [*to* CHOUBERT] You ought to be ashamed of yourself, talking to Monsieur Chief Inspector like that!

DETECTIVE: [*getting into a terrible rage*] I'll teach you to be rude, you poor wretch, you . . . nonentity!

MADELEINE: [*to* DETECTIVE, *who is not listening*] And yet I *am* a good cook, Monsieur. And *he's* got a good appetite! . . .

DETECTIVE: [*to* MADELEINE] You can't teach me anything about medicine, Madame, I know my job. If your son's not falling on his nose, he's always wandering off on his own. He's just not strong enough! We've really got to fatten him up . . .

MADELEINE: [*to* CHOUBERT] You hear what the Doctor says? Think yourself lucky you only fell on your bottom!

DETECTIVE: [*getting more and more furious*] We're no further forward than we were just now! We keep going from top to bottom, from bottom to top, from top to bottom, up and down, round and round, it's a vicious circle!

MADELEINE: [*to* DETECTIVE] I'm afraid he's stuffed with vice! [*In an aggrieved voice, to the* LADY, *who has just come in and remains silent and impassive:*] Isn't he, Madame? [*To* CHOUBERT:] And now I suppose you're going to have the cheek to tell Monsieur Chief Inspector you're not trying to get your own back.

DETECTIVE: I told you before: he's heavy when he ought to be light, too light when he ought to be heavy, he's unbalanced, he's got no grip on reality!

MADELEINE: [*to* CHOUBERT] You've no sense of reality.

CHOUBERT: [*snivelling*] He's had other names too: Marius, Marin, Lougastec, Perpignan, Machecroche . . . His last name was Machecroche! . . .

DETECTIVE: You see, you liar, you're right up to date! But it's *him* we want, the rat. When you get your strength back you'll go and find him. You'll have to learn to go straight to the point. [*To the* LADY:] Won't he, Madame? [*The* LADY *does not reply; anyway, she is not expected to.*] I'll teach you how to avoid wasting time on the way.

MADELEINE: [*to* CHOUBERT] Meanwhile, he's well away, old Machecroche . . . He'll be first, he doesn't waste *his* time, *he's* not lazy.

DETECTIVE: [*to* CHOUBERT] *I'll* give you strength. I'll teach you to do as you're told.

MADELEINE: [*to* CHOUBERT] You must always do as you're told. [*The* DETECTIVE *sits down again and rocks his chair.*]

MADELEINE: [*to the* LADY] Mustn't he, Madame?

DETECTIVE: [*shouting, very loud to* MADELEINE] Are you bringing me coffee, or aren't you?

MADELEINE: Of course I am, Monsieur Chief Inspector! [*She goes towards the kitchen.*]

DETECTIVE: [*to* CHOUBERT] Now it's between us two!

[*At the same moment* MADELEINE *goes out; and at exactly the same time* NICOLAS *comes in through the glass door at the back:* NICOLAS *is tall, with a great black beard, his eyes bleary with sleep, his hair is tousled and his clothes well-worn; he looks like someone who has been asleep in his clothes and has just woken up.*]

NICOLAS: [*coming in*] Hallo!

CHOUBERT: [*in a voice that expresses neither hope, nor fear, nor surprise, but is simply a flat statement*] It's you, Nicolas! You've finished your poem!

[*The* DETECTIVE, *on the other hand, seems very put out by the arrival of this new character; he gives a jump, looks at* NICOLAS *anxiously with rounded eyes, raises himself from his chair and glances at the way out, as if he had a vague idea of flight.*]

CHOUBERT: [*to* DETECTIVE] It's Nicolas d'Eu.

DETECTIVE: [*looking rather wild*] The Tsar of Russia?

CHOUBERT: [*to* DETECTIVE] Oh no, Monsieur, D'Eu is his surname: d apostrophe, e, u. [*To the* LADY *who never replies:*] Isn't it, Madame?

NICOLAS: [*with much gesticulation*] Carry on, carry on, don't let me interrupt you! Don't worry about me!

[*He goes and sits at one side, on the red sofa.* MADELEINE *comes in with a cup of coffee; she seems no longer quite sure who is present. She lays the cup down on the sideboard and goes out again. She repeats this manoeuvre several times, one after the other, without stopping, getting faster and faster and piling up the cups until they cover the whole sideboard.*

Pleased with NICOLAS'S *attitude, the* DETECTIVE *utters a sigh of relief and starts smiling again as he calmly plays at opening and closing his briefcase during the next two short remarks.*]

CHOUBERT: [*to* NICOLAS] Are you pleased with your poem?

NICOLAS: [*to* CHOUBERT] I slept. It's more restful. [*To the imperturbable* LADY:] Isn't i⁻, Madame?

[*The* DETECTIVE *fixes* CHOUBERT *with a stare, crumples a sheet of paper he has taken from his briefcase and throws it on the floor.* CHOUBERT *makes a movement to pick it up.*]

DETECTIVE: [*coldly*] Doesn't matter. Don't pick it up. It's all right where it is. [*Their faces close together, he peers at* CHOUBERT:] I'll give you back your strength. You can't find Mallot, because you've gaps in your memory. We're going to plug those gaps!

NICOLAS: [*slight cough*] Sorry!

DETECTIVE: [*winks at* NICOLAS, *as if they were in league together, then says with servility*] Don't mention it. [*Humbly, still to* NICOLAS:] You're a poet, Monsieur? [*To the impassive* LADY:] He's a poet! [*Then, taking an enormous crust of bread from his briefcase, he offers it to* CHOUBERT:] Eat!

CHOUBERT: I've just had my dinner, Monsieur Chief Inspector, I'm not hungry, I don't eat very much in the evening . . .

DETECTIVE: Eat!

CHOUBERT: I don't feel like it. Really I don't.

DETECTIVE: I'm ordering you to eat, to build up your strength, to plug the gaps in your memory!

CHOUBERT: [*plaintively*] Oh well, if you're going to make me . . . [*Groaning and with a look of disgust he slowly brings the food to his lips.*]

DETECTIVE: Faster, come on, faster, we've lost enough time like this already!

[CHOUBERT *bites, with great difficulty, into the wrinkled old crust.*]

CHOUBERT: It's the bark of a tree, an oak probably. [*To the impassive* LADY:] Isn't it, Madame?

NICOLAS: [*without leaving his place, to the* DETECTIVE] What's your attitude, Monsieur Chief Inspector, to renunciation and detachment?

DETECTIVE: [*to* NICOLAS] One moment . . . So sorry. [*To* CHOUBERT:] It's nice, it's very good for you. [*To* NICOLAS:] My duty, you know, my dear Sir, is simply to apply the system.

CHOUBERT: It's very tough!

DETECTIVE: [*to* CHOUBERT] Come on, no nonsense, don't pull a face, quick, chew!

NICOLAS: [*to* DETECTIVE] You're not just a civil servant, you're also a thinking being! . . . Like the reed . . . You're an individual . . .

DETECTIVE: I am just a soldier, Monsieur . . .

NICOLAS: [*without irony*] I congratulate you.

CHOUBERT: [*groaning*] It's very tough!

DETECTIVE: [*to* CHOUBERT] Chew!

[CHOUBERT *calls to* MADELEINE, *as she rushes in and out setting cups down on the sideboard.*]

CHOUBERT: [*like a child*] Madeleine . . . Madelei-ei-ne . . .

[MADELEINE *goes on rushing in and out, in and out, without taking any notice.*]

DETECTIVE: [*to* CHOUBERT] Leave her alone! [*Conducting the chewing operation by gesture from where he is.*] Can't you move your jaws? Get those jaws working properly!

CHOUBERT: [*weeping*] I'm sorry, Monsieur Chief Inspector, I'm sorry. *Please* forgive me! . . . [*He chews.*]

DETECTIVE: Tears don't have any effect on me.

CHOUBERT: [*continuously chewing*] I've broken my tooth, it's bleeding!

DETECTIVE: Faster, come on, hurry up, chew, chew, swallow!

NICOLAS: I've thought a great deal about the chances of reforming the theatre. Can there be anything new in the theatre? What do you think, Monsieur Chief Inspector?

DETECTIVE: [*to* CHOUBERT] Quick, come on! [*To* NICOLAS:] I don't understand your question.

CHOUBERT: Oouch!

DETECTIVE: [*to* CHOUBERT] Chew!

[MADELEINE's *entries and exits are getting faster and faster.*]

NICOLAS: [*to* DETECTIVE] The theatre of my dreams would be irrationalist.

DETECTIVE: [*to* NICOLAS, *while still keeping an eye on* CHOUBERT] Not Aristotelian, you mean?

NICOLAS: Precisely. [*To the impassive* LADY:] What do you say, Madame?

CHOUBERT: There's no skin left on my palate, and my tongue's all lacerated! . . .

NICOLAS: The contemporary theatre is, indeed, still a prisoner of outmoded forms, it's never got beyond the psychology of a Paul Bourget . . .

DETECTIVE: You've said it! A Paul Bourget! [*To* CHOUBERT:] Swallow!

NICOLAS: You see, my dear fellow, the contemporary theatre doesn't reflect the cultural tone of our period, it's not in harmony with the general drift of the other manifestations of the modern spirit . . .

DETECTIVE: [*to* CHOUBERT] Chew! Swallow! . . .

NICOLAS: It is, however, essential not to lose sight of the new logic, the contributions made by a new kind of psychology . . . a psychology based on antagonism . . .

DETECTIVE: [*to* NICOLAS] Psychology, yes, Monsieur!

CHOUBERT: [*his mouth full*] New . . . psycho . . . lo . . . gy . . .

DETECTIVE: [*to* CHOUBERT] Eat, you! You can talk when you've finished! [*To* NICOLAS:] I'm listening. Theatre that's surreal-izing?

NICOLAS: In so far as surrealism is oneirical . . .

DETECTIVE: [*to* NICOLAS] Oneirical? [*To* CHOUBERT:] Chew, swallow!

NICOLAS: Inspiring me . . . [*To the impassive* LADY:] Right, Madame? [*To* CHOUBERT *again*:] Inspiring me with a different logic and a different psychology, I should introduce contradic-tion where there is no contradiction, and no contradiction where there is what common-sense usually calls contradiction . . . We'll get rid of the principle of identity and unity of character and let movement and dynamic psychology take its place . . . We are not ourselves . . . Personality doesn't exist. Within us there are only forces that are either contradictory or not contradictory . . . By the way, you'd be interested to read LOGIC AND CONTRADICTION, that excellent book by Lupasco . . .

CHOUBERT: [*weeping*] Ouch! Ouch! [*Still chewing and moaning, to* NICOLAS:] You'd get rid of . . . unity . . . like that . . .

DETECTIVE: [*to* CHOUBERT] It's none of your business . . . Eat! . . .

NICOLAS: The characters lose their form in the formlessness of becoming. Each character is not so much himself as another. [*To the impassive* LADY:] Isn't he, Madame?

DETECTIVE: [*to* NICOLAS] So, he'd be more likely to be . . .

[*To* CHOUBERT:] Eat . . . [*To* NICOLAS:] . . . Another than himself ?

NICOLAS: That's obvious. As for plot and motivation, let's not mention them. We ought to ignore them completely, at least in their old form, which was too clumsy, too obvious . . . too phoney, like anything that's too obvious . . . No more drama, no more tragedy: the tragic's turning comic, the comic is tragic, and life's getting more cheerful . . . more cheerful . . .

DETECTIVE: [*to* CHOUBERT] Swallow! Eat . . . [*To* NICOLAS:] I can't say I entirely agree with you . . . though I've a high appreciation for your brilliant ideas . . . [*To* CHOUBERT:] Eat! Swallow! Chew! [*To* NICOLAS:] As for me I remain Aristotelically logical, true to myself, faithful to my duty and full of respect for my bosses . . . I don't believe in the absurd, everything hangs together, everything can be comprehended in time . . . [*To* CHOUBERT:] Swallow! [*To* NICOLAS:] . . . thanks to the achievements of human thought and science.

NICOLAS: [*to the* LADY] What do you think, Madame?

DETECTIVE: I keep moving forward, Monsieur, one step at a time, tracking down the extraordinary . . . I want to find Mallot with a t at the end. [*To* CHOUBERT:] Quick, quick, another piece, come on, chew, swallow!

[MADELEINE'S *entries and exits with the cups get still faster.*]

NICOLAS: You don't agree with me. No hard feelings.

DETECTIVE: [*to* CHOUBERT] Quick, swallow!

NICOLAS: I notice, however, to your credit, that your knowledge of the question is right up-to-date.

CHOUBERT: Madeleine! Madelei-eine!

[*His mouth full and choking, he calls out desperately.*]

DETECTIVE: [*to* NICOLAS] Yes, it's one of my special objects of study. I'm deeply interested . . . But it tires me to think too much about it . . .

[CHOUBERT *bites into the bark again and takes a large piece into his mouth.*]

CHOUBERT: Ouch!

DETECTIVE: Swallow!

CHOUBERT: [*his mouth full*] I'm trying . . . I'm doing . . . my . . . best . . . Can't . . . . do . . . more . . .

NICOLAS: [*to the* DETECTIVE, *who is engrossed in his efforts to get* CHOUBERT *to eat*] Have you also thought about the practical problems of production in this new theatre?

DETECTIVE: [*to* CHOUBERT] Yes, you can! You don't want to! Everybody can! You must *want* to, you can do it all right! [*To* NICOLAS:] I'm sorry, Monsieur, I can't talk about that just now, it's not allowed, I'm on duty!

CHOUBERT: Let me swallow it in little pieces!

DETECTIVE: All right, but faster, faster, faster! [*To* NICOLAS:] We'll discuss it later!

CHOUBERT: [*his mouth full—he has the mental age of a baby of two; he is sobbing*] Ma-ma-ma-de-lei-lei-ne! ! !

DETECTIVE: No nonsense, now! Be quiet! Swallow! [*To* NICOLAS, *who is no longer listening as he is lost in thought:*] He's suffering from anorexia. [*To* CHOUBERT:] Swallow!

CHOUBERT: [*passing his hand across his brow to wipe off the sweat; his stomach is heaving*] Ma-a-de-leine!

DETECTIVE: [*in a yapping voice*] Watch out, whatever you do, don't be sick, it wouldn't get you anywhere, I'd make you swallow it again!

CHOUBERT: [*putting his hand over his ears*] You're splitting my eardrums, Monsieur Inspector . . .

DETECTIVE: [*still shouting*] . . .Chief !

CHOUBERT: [*his mouth full, hands over his ears*] . . . *Chief* Inspector!!

DETECTIVE: Now listen to me carefully, Choubert, listen, leave your ears alone, don't stop them up, or I'll stop them for you, with a clip over the earhole . . .

[*He pulls his hands away by force.*]

NICOLAS: [*who has shown signs, during the last few remarks, of great interest in what is going on*] . . . But . . . but . . . what are you doing, what do you think you're doing?

DETECTIVE: [*to* CHOUBERT] Swallow! Chew! Swallow! Chew! Swallow! Chew! Swallow! Chew! Swallow! Chew! Swallow!

CHOUBERT: [*his mouth full, utters incomprehensible sounds*] Heu . . .
glu . . . you . . . kno . . . clem . . . neeg . . . erls . . .

DETECTIVE: [*to* CHOUBERT] What did you say?

CHOUBERT: [*spitting into his hand what he has in his mouth*] I
wonder if you know? How lovely the columns of the temples
are, and the knees of the young girls!

NICOLAS: [*from his seat, to the* DETECTIVE, *who is still busy with
his job and not listening*] But what are you doing to that child?

DETECTIVE: [*to* CHOUBERT] All this fuss, instead of swallowing
your food! Mustn't talk at table! Snotty-nosed rascal! Ought
to be ashamed! Children should be seen and not heard! Eat
it all up! Quickly!

CHOUBERT: Yes, Monsieur Chief Inspector . . . [*He puts back
into his mouth what he had spat into his hand; then with his mouth
full and his eyes fixed on the* DETECTIVE's:] . . . Ah . . . ee . . .
ay . . . !

DETECTIVE: And now this! . . . [*He stuffs another piece of bread in
his mouth.*] Chew! . . . Swallow! . . .

CHOUBERT: [*making fruitless and painful efforts to chew and swallow*]
. . . oo . . . ire . . .

DETECTIVE: What?

NICOLAS: [*to* DETECTIVE] He says it's wood, and iron. It'll never
go down. Can't you see? [*To the impassive* LADY:] Will it,
Madame?

DETECTIVE: [*to* CHOUBERT] It's only because he wants his own
back!

MADELEINE: [*coming in for the last time to put some more cups on
the table, cups that no one touches or pays any attention to*] Here's
the coffee! Only it's tea!

NICOLAS: [*to* DETECTIVE] The poor child's having a good try,
anyway! Wood and iron, it's all jammed in his throat!

MADELEINE: [*to* NICOLAS] Leave him alone! He can look after
himself, if he wants to!

[CHOUBERT *tries to shout and can't; he is choking.*]

DETECTIVE: [*to* CHOUBERT] Faster, faster, I tell you, swallow it
all at once!

[*Out of patience, the* DETECTIVE *goes to* CHOUBERT, *opens his mouth and prepares to thrust his fist down his throat; he has previously rolled up his sleeve.* NICOLAS *suddenly gets up and approaches the* DETECTIVE, *silently and threateningly, planting himself opposite. The* DETECTIVE *lets go of* CHOUBERT'S *head and leaves him sitting down, gazing at the scene, still silent, still chewing; the* DETECTIVE *is dumbfounded by* NICOLAS's *intervention, and in a voice that is suddenly quite different, quite shaky, he says to* NICOLAS, *almost blubbering:*]

DETECTIVE: Why, Monsieur Nicolas d'Eu, I'm only doing my duty! I didn't come here just to pester him! I've really got to find out where he's hiding, Mallot with a t at the end. There's no other way I can do it. I've no choice. As for your friend—and I hope one day he'll be mine . . . [*He points to the seated* CHOUBERT, *who is looking at them, purple in the face and chewing steadily:*] . . . I respect him, sincerely I do! You, too, my dear Monsieur Nicolas d'Eu. I've often heard about you and your books . . .

MADELEINE: [*to* NICOLAS] Monsieur respects you, Nicolas.

NICOLAS: [*to* DETECTIVE] You're lying!

DETECTIVE AND MADELEINE: Oh! !

NICOLAS: [*to* DETECTIVE] The truth is I'm *not* a writer, and I'm proud of it!

DETECTIVE: [*crushed*] Oh yes, Monsieur, you *do* write! [*In increasing terror:*] Everyone ought to write.

NICOLAS: No point. We've got Ionesco and Ionesco, that's enough!

DETECTIVE: But, Monsieur, there are always things to be said . . . [*He is trembling with fright; to the* LADY:] Aren't there, Madame?

LADY: No! No! Not Madame: Mademoiselle! . . .

MADELEINE: [*to* NICOLAS] Monsieur the Chief Inspector's right. There are always things to be said. Now the modern world's in a state of decay, you can always report on the process!

NICOLAS: [*screaming*] I don't give a damn! . . .

DETECTIVE: [*shaking more and more violently*] But you should, Monsieur!

NICOLAS: [*laughing contemptuously in the* DETECTIVE's *face*] I don't give a damn what you think of me! [*He grips the* DETECTIVE *by his lapels.*] Don't you realize you're mad?

[CHOUBERT *is heroically struggling to chew and swallow. He is contemplating the scene, terrified too. He looks rather guilty. His mouth is too full for him to be able to intervene.*]

MADELEINE: All right, that's enough now, come on . . .

DETECTIVE: [*reaching the limit of indignation and stupefactio , he sits down again, then gets up, knocking his chair over so that it smashes*] Me? Me mad! . . .

MADELEINE: Drink the coffee, then!

CHOUBERT: [*shouting*] I feel all right again! I've swallowed it all! Swallowed it all!

[*During the ensuing conversation, no attention is paid to* CHOUBERT.]

NICOLAS: [*to* DETECTIVE] Yes, you, I mean you! . . .

DETECTIVE: [*bursting into tears*] Oh! . . . It's too much . . . [*Weeping, to* MADELEINE, *who is arranging the cups on the table:*] Thank you, Madeleine, for the coffee! [*Fresh outbreak of tears.*] It's wicked, it's not fair! . . .

CHOUBERT: I'm all right again, I've swallowed it all! Swallowed it all!

[*He is on his feet, hopping and jumping happily round the stage.*]

MADELEINE: [*to* NICOLAS, *whose attitude to the* DETECTIVE *seems to be growing more dangerous*] You're not going to break the laws of hospitality!

DETECTIVE: [*to* NICOLAS, *defending himself*] I didn't want to upset your friend! . . . I swear I didn't! . . . It's *he* who forced *me* to come into this flat . . . *I* didn't want to, I was in a hurry . . . They insisted, both of them . . .

MADELEINE: [*to* NICOLAS] It's the truth!

CHOUBERT: [*continuing as before*] I'm all right now, I swallowed it all, I can go and play!

NICOLAS: [*cruelly and coldly to the* DETECTIVE] Don't deceive yourself. That's not the reason I've got it in for you!

[*This is said in such a tone that* CHOUBERT *stops his frolicking.*]

All movement stops; the characters have their eyes fixed on NICOLAS, *who is in control of the situation.*]

DETECTIVE: [*articulating with difficulty*] But why, then, in Heaven's name? I've done you no harm!

CHOUBERT: Nicolas, I should never have thought you could hate like this.

MADELEINE: [*full of pity for the* DETECTIVE] Poor boy, your big eyes are scorched by all the terror of the earth . . . How white you look . . . now your nice face has lost its composure . . . Poor boy, poor boy! . . .

DETECTIVE: [*terror-stricken*] Did I thank you, Madeleine, for the coffee? [*To* NICOLAS:] I'm only a pawn, Monsieur, a soldier tied to his orders, I'm respectable, honest, a decent chap! . . . And then . . . I'm only twenty, Monsieur! . . .

NICOLAS: [*implacably*] I don't care, I'm forty-five!

CHOUBERT: [*counting on his fingers*] More than twice as old . . . [NICOLAS *takes out a huge knife.*]

MADELEINE: Nicolas, think before you act! . . .

DETECTIVE: Oh God, oh God . . . [*His teeth are chattering.*]

CHOUBERT: He's shivering, he must be cold!

DETECTIVE: Yes, I am cold . . . Ah!

[*He cries out, for* NICOLAS *suddenly brandishes his knife as he moves round him in a circle.*]

MADELEINE: But the radiators are wonderfully hot . . . Nicolas, behave! . . .

[*The* DETECTIVE, *on the point of collapse and in a paroxysm of fear, is making a strange noise.*]

CHOUBERT: [*loudly*] There's a nasty smell . . . [*To the* DETECTIVE:] It's not nice to do it in your trousers!

MADELEINE: [*to* CHOUBERT] But don't you realize what's happening? Put yourself in his place! [*She looks at* NICOLAS.] What a look in his eyes! He's not joking! [NICOLAS *raises his knife.*]

DETECTIVE: Help!

MADELEINE: [*neither her so* CHOUBERT *moving a step*] Nicolas, you've gone all red. Be careful or you'll have an apoplectic fit! Think, Nicolas, you could have been his father!

[NICOLAS *strikes once with his knife and the* DETECTIVE *wheels round and round.*]

CHOUBERT: Too late to stop him . . .

DETECTIVE: [*spinning round*] Long live the white race!

[NICOLAS, *his mouth twisted fiercely, strikes a second time.*]

DETECTIVE: [*still spinning round*] I should like . . . a posthumous decoration.

MADELEINE: [*to* DETECTIVE] You shall have it, my pet. I'll phone the President . . .

[NICOLAS *strikes for the third time.*]

MADELEINE: [*with a start*] Stop it, stop it now! . . .

CHOUBERT: [*reprovingly*] Nicolas, really!

DETECTIVE: [*spinning round for the last time, while* NICOLAS *stands still, his knife in his hand*] I am . . . a victim . . . of duty! . . .

[*Then he crumples into a bloody heap.*]

MADELEINE: [*rushing to the* DETECTIVE'S *body to see if he is dead*] Right through the heart, poor boy! [*To* CHOUBERT *and* NICOLAS:] Help me, then! [NICOLAS *throws aside his bloody knife, then all three, watched by the inscrutable* LADY, *lift the body onto the divan.*] It's such a pity it had to happen in our flat! [*The body is laid on the divan.* MADELEINE *raises the head and slips a pillow under it.*] That's the way! Poor lad . . . [*To* NICOLAS:] We're going to miss him now, this young man you killed . . . Oh, you and your crazy hatred of the police . . . What are we going to do? Who's going to help us find Mallot now? Who? Who?

NICOLAS: Perhaps I was too hasty . . .

MADELEINE: Now you're admitting it; you're all the same . . .

CHOUBERT: Yes, we're all the same . . .

MADELEINE: You act without thinking, and then you're sorry! . . . We've got to find Mallot! His sacrifice [*Indicating the* DETECTIVE:] shall not have been in vain! Poor victim of duty!

NICOLAS: I'll find Mallot for you.

MADELEINE: Well done, Nicolas!

NICOLAS: [*to the* DETECTIVE'S *body*] No, your sacrifice won't have been in vain. [*To* CHOUBERT:] You're going to help me.

CHOUBERT: Oh no, I'm not! I'm not starting that all over again!

MADELEINE: [to CHOUBERT] Haven't you any heart? Surely you can do something for him! [She indicates the DETECTIVE.]

CHOUBERT: [tapping his foot like a sulky child and snivelling] No! I won't! No! I wo-o-on't!

MADELEINE: I don't like husbands who won't do as they're told! What do you mean by it? You ought to be ashamed!

[CHOUBERT is still weeping, but is beginning to look resigned.]

NICOLAS: [sits down in the DETECTIVE's place and holds out to CHOUBERT a piece of bread] Come on, eat, eat, to plug the gaps in your memory!

CHOUBERT: I'm not hungry!

MADELEINE: Haven't you any heart? Do as Nicolas says!

CHOUBERT: [takes the bread and bites into it] It hu-u-urts!

NICOLAS: [in the DETECTIVE's voice] No nonsense! Swallow! Chew! Swallow! Chew!

CHOUBERT: [his mouth full] I'm a victim of duty, too!

NICOLAS: So am I!

MADELEINE: We're all victims of duty! [To CHOUBERT:] Swallow! Chew!

NICOLAS: Swallow! Chew!

MADELEINE: [to CHOUBERT and NICOLAS] Swallow! Chew! Chew! Swallow!

CHOUBERT: [to MADELEINE and NICOLAS, while chewing] Chew! Swallow! Chew! Swallow!

NICOLAS: [to CHOUBERT and MADELEINE] Chew! Swallow! Chew! Swallow!

[The LADY moves towards the other three.]

LADY: Chew! Swallow! Chew! Swallow!

[While all the characters are ordering one another to chew and swallow, the curtain falls.]

CURTAIN

September 1952